Creating a Mentoring Program

Mentoring Partnerships Across the Generations

Annabelle Reitman
Sylvia Ramirez Benatti

ASTD PRESS

ASTD Press is an internationally renowned source of insightful and practical information on workplace learning, performance, and professional development.

ASTD Press
1640 King Street Box 1443
Alexandria, VA 22313-1443 USA

Ordering information: Books published by ASTD Press can be purchased by visiting ASTD's website at store.astd.org or by calling 800.628.2783 or 703.683.8100.

Library of Congress Control Number: 2014934636

ISBN-10: 1-56286-898-5
ISBN-13: 978-1-56286-898-7
e-ISBN: 978-1-60728-404-8

ASTD Press Editorial Staff:
Director: Glenn Saltzman
Manager and Editor, ASTD Press: Ashley McDonald
Community of Practice Manager, Human Capital: Ann Parker
Editorial Assistant: Ashley Slade
Text Design: Lon Levy and Bernard Bello
Cover Design: Marisa Kelly

Printed by Data Reproductions Corporation, Auburn Hills, MI, www.datarepro.com

Contents

Preface

The Mentoring Partnership Model has been in the making since 2009, when we began to reflect about the existing generations in the workplace and what this means for organizational activities and productivity. This thinking led to our presentation, "Sustaining Engagement and Succession Planning Through Intergenerational Conversations" at the 2009 ASTD International Conference & Exposition. Reactions from the audience encouraged and reinforced our ideas that generational relationships were changing. This was the onset of what eventually became the Mentoring Partnerships Model.

As we continued to give presentations, for the Metro DC ASTD Chapter, Chesapeake Bay Organizational Development Network, and Alexandria Women's Network (among others), on all or parts of the "intergenerational conversations" presentation, we could visualize a greater and broader concept and impact. From the exercises, Who Do You Think I Am? and Who I Am! and Intergenerational Communication Skills we received in-depth feedback, particularly on how much the different generations wanted to learn from each other.

As a result, we had a number of discussions about bringing the generations together for equal opportunities to learn. Another influential factor was our experience as past Metro DC ASTD Chapter presidents, of hearing from senior members how tired they were of always being expected to mentor and share their knowledge. They too wanted the opportunity to be engaged in learning as a benefit of being a chapter member. This reinforced our findings on the generations; Boomers and Traditionalists continually want to learn, develop a better understanding of the younger generations, and stay current with the latest technology.

In creating the communication skills exercise for intergenerational conversations, extensive review was done on the generations: who they are, how they communicate, what are the similarities and differences, and so on. We also researched mentoring programs, learning styles, and communications between the generations. Interestingly, little reference was found regarding the importance of differences in communication and learning styles as having an impact on the mentoring process.

We learned that a third party, for example HR, usually establishes the traditional matching process in a mentoring program. It is difficult to determine personalities or synergy from this method, in which feedback from the participants is used to identify the best possible match. In contrast, the Mentoring Partnership Model provides a process that enables the participants to conduct their own matching process to identify compatible mentor partners.

The exercise Who Do You Think I Am? and Who I Am! was the foundation for the What Do I Want to Teach or Share? and What Do I Want to Learn? ones. We knew from our own experience and knowledge as a career coach and a trainer that communication was critical to a viable and successful mentoring partnership. Essential to the model is providing background on generational communications and creating an exercise to identify each participant's communication style. A pilot program was conducted with the Metro DC Chapter of ASTD, whereby participants provided valuable hands-on prospective that helped us to further refine the delivery process.

The first handout created for the pilot program was a short participant's workbook, which has evolved into two documents: A Coordinator's Manual and a Participant's Workbook. These products are the basis for The Mentoring Partnership Guide and The Mentoring Partner's Workbook, containing complete procedural steps, activities, exercises, and assessments. Materials also include guidelines for successful mentoring partnership meetings and relationships. We hope that our goal has been met—that by using our product, an organization is able to implement a Mentoring Partnership Program, from announcing the program to recruiting participants to the closing celebration.

We would like to acknowledge the forward-thinking people who have chosen to adapt our nontraditional mentoring model for their organization or association. The willingness of your senior level executives or boards is also recognized for having an open mindset to new ideas and approaches. It is hoped that you and the participants find the experience to be as exciting and worthwhile as we have envisioned.

We want to express our appreciation to ASTD Press staff for their support and encouragement in writing the Guide and Workbook and giving us this opportunity to realize our goal and dream.

Annabelle and Sylvia

Part I

The Mentoring Partnership Guide

Chapter 1

Introduction

If you enter "mentoring" in the search engine of a major online bookseller, you will receive 10,261 results. By adding the word "business" and narrowing the search, you will still have 263 results. Mentoring in a great variety of arenas appears to be a very hot topic, but why? Ensher and Murphy (2005) pointed out that it seems like a fad, here today and gone tomorrow, along with all of the help books and hype. But we would argue that it's here to stay, and adds true value. Mentoring can be a great tool to prepare the next generation of leaders, share intellectual capital, pass on organizational history, and engage employees or members in an organization.

The Organization's Overall Perspective

When your organization considers the initiation of a mentoring program, the first set of questions that needs to be asked is: What are our expectations and goals for this program? Will a mentoring program's purpose be aligned with the organization's objectives? How will this program tie into the organization's strategy for its employees or members' development and its succession planning?

Senior Leadership's Perspective

The next set of questions is focused on the organization's senior leadership and support for the program. Does the senior leadership understand the benefits of a mentoring program? What do they see as the value-added asset of having this additional learning opportunity available? How can they be made aware of the importance of their support? With their endorsement of a mentoring program's proposal, other people such as managers, directors, and staff will follow. However, if the attitude is that this is nice to have but not necessary, then others may not be as willing to give their time and effort to be involved in this activity.

Employees' or Members' Perspective

The last set of questions is regarding the organization's employees or members and their concerns. Would they want a mentoring program to be offered? How do they see this activity as a benefit to their development and growth? Are they able and willing to commit a certain minimum amount of time to their participation? Today, mentoring is a commonplace involvement; however, it means something different to different people. In addition, it cannot be assumed that everyone knows or understands the merits of a mentoring relationship. Employees or members need to be fully aware that an agreement is formalized and commit to at least a six-month period to have a worthwhile experience.

A Mentoring Program's Essential Elements
The Matching Process

A screening process needs to be developed for application to the program. The extent of any qualifying criteria for candidates should be at the discretion of the organization. The senior leaders of the organization should know the composition of their employees or members and who can benefit from participating in a mentoring relationship. Criteria should be established prior to the start of the program.

There are a number of options for accomplishing the matching procedure. They include: 1) a formal method of pairing candidates whereby a third party, usually the human resources department, reviews the submitted application forms and determines appropriate matches from the information received; and 2) informal networks where one hopes to connect with a suitable person to establish a mentoring relationship.

The Mentoring Partnership Model offers a nontraditional matching option—a self-selection process—where participants identify what they want to learn and what they can teach, and with the exchange of the information independently match themselves. Finding the appropriate match is critical to the success of a mentoring experience. Beyond the mutual learning that takes place, the existing synergy or chemistry between the partners contributes to the depth of the experience.

In a traditional mentoring relationship, one individual gains knowledge and guidance while the other person gains the opportunity to give back to a professional community or build a legacy within the organization. However, the Mentoring Partnership Model allows for mutual learning and active involvement for both partners. Therefore, an organization will have its history and intellectual capital passed on to the next generation, keep employees or members (both senior and junior) retained and engaged, and potentially identify candidates for their succession schedule.

Feedback and Evaluation

Ongoing feedback and evaluation are equally important to both the participating individuals and the organization. Feedback is a crucial communication tool between partners, between the program coordinator and partners, and to follow up with organization leadership. An open, honest, and accepting dialogue in a mentoring relationship is vital to the individual's growth and to the quality of the learning accomplished. Understanding how to deliver and receive feedback are skills that an individual can apply to other situations.

An evaluation process helps to determine if goals have been achieved. To keep the process on track and the goals focused, structured interim evaluations of the program's activities and management are recommended. A final evaluation indicates the rate of success, the specific areas where it has been accomplished, and to how the goals were ultimately met.

For the program coordinator and the organization, feedback and evaluation are equally important. The coordinator needs to know about his performance level—what was carried out well and where improvements are needed. Everyone needs to know if the program went as envisioned; whether goals were met, unrealistic, or not suitable; and if additions or changes are needed. Specific strengths and weaknesses are reviewed to learn what successes can be replicated and decide where improvements are necessary. Everyone involved in the program, from senior leadership to participants, should contribute to a list of lessons learned.

Taking all of these points into consideration is very important for establishing a mentoring program that benefits the individual participants and the organization. Mentoring programs can be a great asset to an organization, whether through the traditional model or the partnership model. They can increase engagement and retention of employees or members. Professional development can be provided across the organization, to share and retain valuable intellectual capital. In addition, a mentoring program also demonstrates how the company or organization values its employees and their professional and personal growth.

Basic Characteristics of Mentoring

Traditionally in a mentoring relationship, a senior-level person provides guidance, support, and information for a younger person just beginning her career. Today, with several generations in leadership and workplace situations, diverse communications and professional styles are exhibited. Participants need to be authentic, open minded, and have empathy for other points of view in order to understand the challenges and opportunities that can be encountered in a mentoring relationship. Cross-generational mentoring is happening more frequently—people are acknowledging that everyone can benefit from assistance in some area and that everyone has some wisdom to exchange. Just growing up in different eras and seeing the world through different lenses can contribute to shared insights. In accepting this perspective, people are able to move their mentoring experience forward and have successful and rewarding interactions.

There are many types and styles of mentoring. Regardless of the model or form the mentoring program takes, each has comparable goals and objectives to help the participants increase knowledge, skills, and capacity. The basic purpose includes:

- developing skills and competencies for future career plans and professional capability

- exploring future career direction and work options

- providing a sounding board to listen and to ask the difficult question

- sharing life experiences, specifically those dealing with new or difficult situations

- giving support and encouragement to seek new challenges, not become discouraged, and persevere.

The difference is in how these components are combined, integrated, and put into action—their *modus operandi*. In a traditional model, the majority of these elements go one way—down toward the junior or younger employee or member, the mentee. In a partnership model, all elements apply equally to each individual.

Characteristics of an Effective Mentor

Effective mentors are willing to commit to building productive and strong working relationships with their partner. They support the workplace values, mission, and goals. They bring their own unique organizational history and experience to a mentoring approach. In a traditional mentoring relationship, the mentor acts as role model.

Successful participants involved in a mentoring relationship are able and willing to:

- Spend meaningful time in focused give and take discussions.

- Create an environment that is comfortable for being open and honest about views, feelings, and opinions.

- Share knowledge about the organization and its "way of doing things."

- Make introductions to people who can assist in achieving short-term professional and long-term career goals.

- Check periodically to ensure that expectations of both parties are in sync and realistic regarding the existing relationship.

- Allow feelings of frustration to be expressed and give candid and constructive feedback.

- Encourage the testing of new waters, trying out different roles, and practicing new skills.

- Follow through on agreements made.

- Provide access to informal communication networks.

- Expand opportunities for visibility.

- Review career objectives and plans for their achievement and offer suggestions for improvement.

- Reinforce "lessons learned" when failure occurs and that risk is OK.

- Celebrate achievements and successes.

Qualified participants for a mentoring relationship are:

- enthusiastic about another's dreams and aspirations

- motivating and encouraging about the other person's new challenges, changes, or difficulties

- open to sharing their experience with the other person about similar concerns, issues, or encounters

- empathic toward another's feelings, ideas, and outlook

- supportive toward the other's needs and concerns

- objective regarding the other person's solutions and action plans.

Productive mentoring results in experiences that are quite rewarding, educational, enriching, and appreciated by both parties.

The Mentoring Partnership Approach

The Mentoring Partnership Model is distinctive because it is intentionally designed and planned to build relationships that provide two-way inclusive interactions exchanging insights, knowledge, and expertise, which result in mutual learning benefits for both participants regardless of generational or workplace status. The diversity of our generations, cultures, and experiences bring so many learning opportunities to the table. Why limit the learning to only one side of the conversation? In today's society we say that we value diversity because it emboldens creativity and opens more ways to bring new ideas. Why shouldn't this apply to taking advantage of promoting individual and community learning? Why not use what we value—the diversity of knowledge and experience—to broaden our development?

As mentioned in the preface, the design of the Mentoring Partnership Model is based on the interactions we saw between the generations in our intergenerational conversation exercises. We saw their interest in what the other generation could teach them. Creating an environment that values what individuals contribute to the development of their colleagues enhances self-esteem and self-confidence. When someone comes to you to learn from you, this enhances your own feelings of self-worth. Too many times we (the senior members) determine that we must teach the junior. While there is always something to learn, do we acknowledge that the junior has knowledge that we could learn from? And also, if we seem to always be designated as the ones who must give and share knowledge, when do we learn?

This model provides a structure enabling two members of separate age groups to work as a team, assisting each other to improve and expand their strengths for themselves and their organizational success. This relationship involves a "give-and-take" style whereby people feel free and comfortable to express ideas and suggestions, ask for help, voice disagreements, and so forth. It is a connection whereby two people see themselves as colleagues bringing compatible learning styles and desired skills, experience, and knowledge to the relationship. A Mentoring Partnership team is an equitable association that connects two individuals bringing talents, skills, and experiences to the table, which the other person wants to acquire. Examples of learning that can occur include: passing on the organization's story, imparting technical skills, exchanging generational characteristics, advising how to fit into the organization's culture, and exchanging job skills across departments.

Individual and Organization Benefits

The participants involved in a Mentoring Partnership Program and the organization sponsoring the program benefit from it. Thus, it is a "win-win" situation enhancing both the individuals and the organization. Individual benefits:

- Receive desired customized learning in a one-on-one situation, convenient in time, place, and method.

- Create new and stronger bonds among colleagues.

- Expand knowledge, insights, and expertise in organizational, personal, and professional arenas as a two-way learning exchange.

- Develop larger professional networks by having access to a new range of contacts made possible by a mentoring partner.

Organization benefits:

- Inspire new talent to identify with the organization and its culture by building stronger ties and working relationships.

- Retain the engagement of senior-level members with opportunities to learn while passing on their legacies.

- Sustain engagement and prevent loss of emerging talent.

- Enhance leadership and succession planning.

To establish and build an effective and successful mentor partnership, guidelines and support resources are needed. This Guide (part I) provides the information, format, and exercises to plan, initiate, and coordinate a Mentoring Partnership Program for nonprofit/community-related, business/for-profit, and government employers. The Workbook (part II) introduces the participants to the program and discusses recommendations and tips for developing a meaningful and productive working relationship.

Flexibility of Venues

In addition to the workplace, this model can be applied in other arenas as well. Some examples include:

- Elementary through high school education: Senior-level and first-year teachers can form partnerships. First-year teachers have new and innovative techniques by virtue of being recent graduates; senior teachers have hands-on experience in the classroom and in the system.

- Higher education: Tenured faculty can learn the latest teaching trends and tools from junior faculty; while junior faculty can learn about the tenure process and its requirements.

- Trade and professional associations: Being a member of an association allows for opportunities to build relationships across the generations, resulting in continuous learning for senior members and for junior members as they gain networking possibilities and knowledge.

As mentioned previously, one specific and unique audience in professional associations are their senior members, who wish to continue to benefit from their membership as well as to continue to contribute to the association's value. Therefore, it's essential to be proactive in recruiting the more experienced and active members for involvement by stressing the two-way learning and exchange that will take place.

Chapter 2

Overview of Model Format

It is important for participants to realize that they are not operating as a lone mentoring partnership, but are involved in an organizational program where people share concerns, experiences, and support. The process starts with an orientation meeting where mentoring partnerships are formed, and closes with a celebration event where participants can review their experiences, provide feedback, and reinforce their successes.

Preparation Planning

Like most well-run initiatives, proper planning is critical to the long-term success of the program and the participants. The process for promotion and recruitment should begin no less than two months prior to the orientation. (See chapter 8 for sample materials.) Also during this time, logistics can be arranged for the location, catering, and ordering workbooks.

Once the participants are identified, the program facilitator needs to be prepared to send both the orientation registration information form and the matching process exercise to the participants. It is critical that the matching process exercise be sent in advance of the orientation to give the participants the opportunity to reflect and identify what they want to give to and gain from a mentoring partnership connection.

Group Meetings

Meetings are scheduled throughout the six-month program cycle for administrative purposes and to develop a sense of community. They begin with an orientation, followed by a launch session, a mid-point review, and a celebration program to evaluate and close the program.

Orientation: Matching Process and Initiating Partnerships

A Mentoring Partnership Program begins with an orientation meeting for those who have expressed an interest in participating. The purpose is to introduce and discuss this mentoring approach, its goals, the six-month commitment, and the benefits of a self-matching mentoring partnership. Orientation is scheduled as a one-day meeting or as two-half day meetings; when split into two days, the second one is held within a week of the first. Prior to the meeting, prospective participants complete forms identifying at least three things they want to learn and three things they are willing to teach or share in a two-way experience. The completed forms are brought to the orientation. This information is posted around the room so that all the participants are able to review what each person is offering and needs. After identifying a potential match, participants will have a brief conversation to determine if an initial partnership selection has been made. More than one conversation can occur to determine if two people have a potential partnership.

Note: It is critical that attendees are aware that matches may not occur for everyone—there are no guarantees.

After initial matches are made, the orientation continues with those who have been matched, to distribute Partner's Workbooks, which will include a Mentoring Partnership Agreement. These tools help partner teams to continue their conversations and make plans to meet and become better acquainted. This is also an opportunity for the group to form a cohort community designed to provide each mentoring partnership team a community of mutual support.

Program Launch

About three weeks after orientation, the formal start of a program cycle is held. Prior to the meeting, potential partners will have connected to reconfirm their compatibility and expectations for this relationship. The Mentoring Partnership Agreement has been completed, signed, and brought to the meeting, initiating the establishment of the partnership and commitment to a six-month rotation.

Mid-Point Review

This meeting provides participants with a sense of community and support for their journey. They can check in with other partnerships to compare and share experiences, develop their concerns and issues, and have their questions answered. The coordinator begins to learn how the program is going and if any partnerships need individual follow-up to strengthen the mentoring relationship.

Closing Celebration and Evaluation

When the six-month commitment is completed, a celebration gives participants a sense of accomplishment and recognition of their achievement. It allows participants to give feedback, improvement suggestions, and bring closure to this six-month period. A summary is given regarding how the leadership and coordinator viewed the results of the program. A formal evaluation form is emailed to participants, completed and signed individually, and returned. Additionally, partnerships can decide to continue beyond this rotation.

Mentor Partnership Agreement

An agreement helps to ensure accountability between the partners and to the Mentoring Partnership Program, and avoids misunderstandings. A completed and signed copy is given to the coordinator.

Program Timeline

The timeline for the entire process from start to finish is approximately 10 months, as follows:

- Three months: Pre-program planning, which includes promotion, recruiting, and logistics.

- Six months: Implementation of the program.

- One month: Celebration occurs at the end of the six month period—allow one month prior to the event for preparation.

- One month: Submit final report of the outcomes.

Chapter 3

Mentoring Partnership Program Orientation

The orientation introduces the concepts and process of the Mentoring Partnership Model. The first half of the meeting is held to present an overview of the program and conduct the matching process for potential partners. The second half of the orientation is the initiating or beginning of the partnership process. There are two delivery options: one full-day meeting or two half-days.

- A full-day format allows for immediate, continued bonding between two potential partners; it enables a growing commitment to the program.

- If two half-days are held, it's recommended they're not more than a week apart. Potential partners are encouraged, in-between the meetings, to have an extended conversation to confirm the compatibility of the match.

Prior to orientation, the following activities should be completed:

- Prospective participants will complete a registration form (see a sample on page 27).

- Participants will receive an acknowledgment of registration and orientation meeting details.

- Three weeks prior to the orientation participants will receive the What Do I Want to Learn? and What Do I Want to Teach or Share? exercises (samples on pages 29-30). Participants will complete these exercises and bring them to the orientation, as they are necessary for the partnership matching process.

- A week before the orientation date, attendees will receive a reminder regarding the scheduled event and to bring their completed exercise forms.

Mentoring Partnership Program Orientation

The mentoring partnership process is about mutual learning. Age, position, or even years of experience do not decide who the mentor is in a mentoring partnership. Each partner brings a desire to learn something new and a particular piece of knowledge to teach. The first part of the orientation will include introductions and the matching activities.

Introductions

The welcome and introduction of participants is the first step in the orientation. Introductions can include asking participants to share their expectations or what they hope to gain from the experience. To help people become better acquainted and begin bonding, icebreakers can be facilitated by forming small groups and asking them to complete the following sentence: "I am a member of _____ generation and what most defines me as a member of my generation is _____." Responses can then be shared with the group at large. (A sample handout for this exercise is included at the end of this section on page 31.)

Then an overview of the Mentoring Partnership Model and the goals and objectives of the program are provided.

Matching Process

The matching process begins with participants taking out their completed exercise forms and reviewing them one last time. They are then asked to transfer this information, along with their names, to the paper that is taped up around the room. One section of paper is titled What Do You Want to Learn? and the other is titled What Can You Teach or Share? Participants' responses and identifying initials are placed under the appropriate title.

Note: As people check in and pick up their nametags and other materials, check if they have brought their completed exercise. If the forms are not fully completed, explain that they need to do so before the matching process officially begins.

Identify Partners

The participants review all the postings to identify the individual or potential individuals who are offering to teach or share the information they want to learn. Once a tentative match has been identified, a brief conversation is held (suggested topics on page 32) to determine whether there is a possible match. After the first round, it is feasible to conduct a second round, as there may still be some unmatched people or people who want to talk to other potential partners.

Note: Some people may not be partnered. Therefore, it is critical to manage unrealistic expectations that everyone will find a match from the outset of the process. There are no guarantees.

The conclusion of the matching process ends the first part of orientation. If some people were not matched it should be explained that they can reapply for the next orientation meeting and that a follow-up email will be sent to them.

Initiating the Partnership

The second half of orientation can either follow a lunch break or be conducted as a separate meeting within a week of the first session. During this portion of the session, copies of the Partner's Workbook are distributed to the matched teams. To help the new mentoring partnership teams become better acquainted, partners are asked to complete the exercises regarding their communication preferences, followed by a group discussion to share what was learned.

Open Workbook to review the Mentoring Partnership Agreement and inform the group that they will also receive a copy via email.

The purpose of the Partnership Agreement is to help ensure accountability between the partners and to the Mentoring Program by laying ground rules, defining boundaries, and establishing goals and a work plan. Participants are able to avoid misunderstandings about desired learning outcomes and outline strategies and work plans for creating and strengthening a successful mentoring relationship. This written and signed agreement brings realistic baselines to mentoring activities and end results. (A sample Mentoring Partnership Agreement is included on page 39.)

Elements of the Agreement

In the Mentoring Partnership Agreement, partners should be able to work out the following to the satisfaction of both individuals:

- well-defined goals

- a work plan for learning activities and tools used

- success criteria and measurement

- ground rules for a positive, harmonious relationship

- boundaries and barriers

- procedures for handling stumbling blocks

- accountability and review of the mentoring partnership progress.

Differences of opinions, definitions, procedures, and so on, should be approached with professionalism, respect, and a certain amount of give and take.

Closing Remarks

An announcement is given for the program launch meeting date, time, and location. Partners are encouraged to carefully review the Workbook during their first meeting before completing the Mentoring Partnership Agreement. The Workbook explains that a copy of the completed, signed agreement will need to be brought to the program launch meeting (or sent to the coordinator by a certain date).

Orientation Meeting Delivery Process

The orientation can be a one-or two-day event. A one-day event allows the participants to move from identifying their potential partner to beginning to develop a relationship with activities designed to foster the relationship and to explain the how the process works. A two-day event allows the potential partners to meet between the first half-day meeting and the second to begin developing their relationship.

Orientation Meeting Part I: Half-Day Format
Meeting Goals

- Introduce interested members to the Mentoring Partnership Program: its operational process, goals, benefits, and how the matching process works.

- Conduct the matching process to identify potential pairings for the program.

Materials, Handouts, and Forms

The facilitator requires the following materials:

- the annotated agenda

- instructions for the My Generation icebreaker

- overview of the mentoring partnership philosophy and history

- description of the What Do I Want to Learn? What Do I Want to Teach or Share? activity

- Orientation Part I Evaluation

- poster paper, butcher paper, or newsprint and colored markers.

The following handouts or forms are found at the end of this section (pages 27-34):

- Registration and Sign-In Form

- Follow-Up Cover Letter to Potential Participants' Initial Inquiry

- What Do I Want to Learn? Exercise

- What Do I Want to Teach or Share? Exercise

- My Generation Orientation Icebreaker

- Example of Poster Paper Layout

- Discussion Questions to Confirm Match

- Orientation Part I: The Matching Process Evaluation (also found in the Workbook).

Preparation

For Facilitators

Three months prior to meeting, the following tasks must be completed:

- Schedule the date of orientation meeting.

- Determine if orientation parts I and II will be delivered on separate days or on the same day.

- Identify the location and reserve space.

- Develop a promotional plan (for example, flyers, newsletters, and social media).

- Recruit interested participants.

One month prior to meeting:

- Send confirmation to participants.

- Confirm room setup and food (optional).

Two weeks prior to meeting:

- Send participants the What Do I Want to Learn? and What Do I Want to Teach or Share? exercises with instructions explaining its purpose and that it needs to be completed and brought to the meeting.

- Send participants the meeting agenda.

- Prepare the meeting handout (the icebreaker activity).

- Have extra copies of the What Do I Want to Learn? and What Do I Want to Teach or Share? exercises available for the orientation in case they are needed.

For Participants

One month prior to meeting:

- Send email or letter confirming participation in the Mentoring Program orientation meeting.

Two weeks prior to meeting:

- Complete the What Do I Want to Learn? and What Do I Want to Teach or Share? exercises, following the instructions. The exercises must be completed prior to the meeting and brought to the meeting.

Half-Day Agenda

Orientation Part I: 3.5-hour meeting.

30 minutes   Registration and coffee.

- Confirm that participants have completed and brought a copy of the What Do I Want to Learn? and What Do I Want to Teach or Share? exercises.

- If any participant does not have them provide blank forms to be completed prior to the matching process.

45 minutes   Welcome and introduction of attendees:

- Sample My Generation icebreaker activity: attendees share their name, generation, how they reflect their generation, and their expectations of being involved in a Mentoring Partnership Program or describe how they hope to benefit from the experience.

15 minutes   Overview of the Mentoring Partnership Program:

- Provide the definition, goals, objectives, and benefits of the program, as well as how it will operate.

10 minutes   Break:

- At this time, if you have any participants who still need to complete the What Do I Want to Learn? and What Do I Want to Teach or Share? exercises have them complete them during the break.

35 minutes   Describe how the matching process will work:

- Review the What Do I Want to Learn? and What Do I Want to Teach or Share? exercises. Ask if there are any questions or concerns about completing them.

- Transfer the responses to the What Do I Want to Learn? and What Do I Want to Teach or Share? exercises to paper taped around the room. Divide the paper between three separate sections, giving each a topic (such as Professional Development, Personal Development, or Association/Community Volunteerism). Put at least one sheet of paper each for What Do I Want to Learn? and What Do I Want to Teach or Share? in each section. (See the sample diagram on page 32.)

1 hour   Complete the matching activity:

- Ask attendees to go around and review the postings to identify the potential individual(s) who are offering to teach or share the information, skill, or resource they want to learn or know about.

- When a tentative match has been determined, the attendees conduct a brief conversation to confirm if compatibility does exist and a potential match has been made.

- If there appears to be more than one possible match for all or some of the attendees, then a second round of conversations are conducted.

15 minutes   Review the tentative partnership matches:

- Introduce tentative matches to the group with brief remarks on why the individuals think they have made a match.

- Part I is concluded. Those who have identified a partner reconvene following a lunch break (or another day) for Part II: Initiating the Partnership.

- Complete Orientation Part I Evaluation.

If a separate second meeting is selected:

- Announce the date of the second part of the orientation.

- Let participants know they will receive a follow-up email within 48 hours with the Mentoring Partnership Agreement.

- Remind partners to schedule at least one face-to-face meeting before the next meeting.

Facilitator notes:

- It is critical from the outset of the process to state several times that matches are not guaranteed and there may be attendees who will not be able to participate in the program.

- A member of the committee should be assigned to speak with those participants who do not find a match. Provide them with follow-up information regarding the next six-month rotation and information for whom to contact if they're interested in trying again next time.

- Record members' names for each formed partnership.

Mentoring Partnership Orientation Registration and Sign-in Form							
Participants		Contact Information		Initial inquiry	Reg. Info and Exercise	Orientation Sign in	Identified Partner
Last Name	First Name	Email	Phone	Date Received	Date Sent	Date Received	Name/Initials	Name

Sample: Follow-Up Cover Letter
to Potential Participants' Initial Inquiry

Dear **NAME:**

We are delighted to learn of your interest in the new **COMPANY'S OR ORGANIZATION'S** Mentoring Partnership Program. Traditionally, in a mentoring relationship, a senior-level person provides guidance, support, and information for a younger person just beginning their career pathway. We are offering a new perspective whereby a mentoring partnership is established as a two-way inclusive interaction with an exchange of knowledge and expertise providing mutual learning benefits for both.

This new program is launching with an orientation meeting on **DATE** and **TIME**, at **LOCATION**. We will facilitate the orientation, conduct the matching process, and coordinate the cohort of mentoring partners.

The registration form for the orientation is attached, please complete it and return via email to **EMAIL**. You will receive a confirmation that your registration has been received and a packet with the details for the orientation and pre-meeting exercises What Do I Want to Learn? and What Do I Want to Teach or Share? It is essential that the exercises be completed prior to attending the orientation and that you bring them to the orientation. These exercises are the foundation of the matching process. By the orientation's conclusion, mentoring partnerships will be identified. Please note it may not be possible to match everyone at this time.

We hope you will join us to learn more about this exciting and innovative program. For further information and to RSVP please respond to **EMAIL** by **DATE**.

Looking forward to meeting you!

NAME
Coordinator

Note: Attach the registration form to the cover letter.

What Do I Want to Learn?
Exercise

Instructions: Please list the topics or areas that you would like to learn more about. Write each item under one of the categories. Please bring the completed form with you to the orientation.

PROFESSIONAL	ASSOCIATION/COMMUNITY	PERSONAL DEVELOPMENT

What Do I Want to Teach or Share?
Exercise

Instructions: Please list the topics or areas that you would like to share with, or teach to, another person. Write each item under one of the categories. Please bring this completed form with you to the orientation.

PROFESSIONAL	ASSOCIATION/COMMUNITY	PERSONAL DEVELOPMENT

My Generation
Orientation Icebreaker

Please tell us your name, your generation, how you are a reflection of your generation, and what you want to gain from a Mentoring Partnership.

Example of Poster Paper Layout

Professional Development		Association/Community		Personal Development	
What do I want to teach or share?	What do I want to learn?	What do I want to teach or share?	What do I want to learn?	What do I want to teach or share?	What do I want to learn?

Discussion Questions to Confirm Match

The following are potential questions to trigger a conversation confirming you have a match.

- Would you tell me more about _____?
- Would you like me to explain or give you more information about_____?
- What was your experience regarding _____?

Orientation Part I: The Matching Process
Evaluation

Thank you for participating in the opening of your organization's Mentoring Partnership Program. In order for us to provide the very best experience, we are committed to continuous improvement and this can only be accomplished with your feedback. Please complete the following brief survey.

Please rate the following responses from 1 (not at all effective), 2 (somewhat effective), 3 (neutral), 4 (effective), to 5 (very effective); include a brief explanation.

1. How valuable was the promotion of the program? _____

   _____

2. Overall, how effective was part I of the orientation? _____

   _____

3. How effective were the teach and learn exercises for helping you identify your goals? _____

   _____

4. How effective was the process of posting and then reviewing other participants teach
   and learn aspirations? _____

   _____

5. How effective was the matching process? _____

   _____

Please briefly answer the following questions.

1. What went well?

   _____

   _____

   _____

2. How can it be improved?

_____

_____

_____

Additional comments:

_____

_____

_____

Part II: Initiating the Partnership

Following the first part of the orientation meeting, which ends in the tentative identification of mentor partners, there are two options for finalizing matched pairs process:

- The second part of the orientation takes place following a lunch break (for the full-day meeting).

- The second part of the orientation takes place on a separate day (for the half-day meeting).

The program's coordinator is responsible for deciding whether the orientation will be a one- or two-day event. She should take into account input from other relevant organization/association groups for example, HRD department staff, or chapter board members, and applicants for the program.

Meeting Goals

- Paired individuals become better acquainted.

- Distribute and review the Mentoring Partner's Workbooks.

- Clarify the Mentoring Partnership Agreement.

- Begin to develop mentoring partnership cohort community.

- Explain the next steps and set the launch meeting.

Materials, Handouts, and Forms

The facilitator requires the following materials:

- the Mentoring Partner's Workbooks

- handouts (found in the Workbook).

The following handouts or forms are found at the end of this section (pages 38-42) and in the Partner's Workbook:

- Are You Ready for a Mentoring Relationship? Exercise

- Mentoring Partnership Agreement

- Orientation Part II: Initiating the Partnership Evaluation.

Preparation

Before the meeting is held, the facilitators should do the following:

- For one-day meeting: arrange for lunch if it's to be included, or provide a list of nearby restaurants.

- For two-day meeting: arrange for a location, and send participants a copy of the Mentoring Partnership Agreement.

Agenda

15 minutes	Arrange the room so that tentative partners are seated together and then facilitate a review of part I of the orientation meeting.
30 minutes	Review the Are You Ready for Mentoring Relationship? exercise: • Ask each individual team to join with two other teams. • Distribute the exercise. • Have each group reflect on the questions and discuss the benefits and concerns being ready for a mentoring partnership. • Have each group report a summary of their discussions.
20 minutes	Open Workbook to review the Partner's Workbook.
30 minutes	Distribute and review the Mentoring Partnership Agreement: • Discuss each item of the agreement.

- Identify individual learning goals

- What is the criteria for success, how will you know that learning has been accomplished, and how will it be measured?

- What is the work plan for accomplishing the goals and what are your target dates?

- What are your ground rules for working, communicating, and learning together?

- Address and think of "what if" scenarios.

- Have partner teams begin to review how they will complete each segment of the agreement.

30 minutes
- Introduce and discuss how the partners will implement their mentoring partnership.

- Set the date for the launch meeting (it should be held within two weeks of this meeting).

- Complete Orientation Part II: Initiating the Partnership Evaluation

Are You Ready for a Mentoring Relationship?
Exercise

The purpose of this review is to help you determine if you are ready for a mentoring relationship. The questions will help you evaluate yourself and your motivation. Please circle the appropriate answer.

1. Do you believe a mentor would be of help to your growth at this time?   Yes   No

2. Are you willing to commit the time, energy, and resolve needed for a successful mentoring relationship?   Yes   No

3. Are you ready to learn, listen, and ask questions?   Yes   No

4. Are you willing to hear and accept feedback and to give equally productive feedback?   Yes   No

5. Are you ready to develop an open, honest, and transparent relationship committed to achieving the goals of a mentoring partnership?   Yes   No

6. Are you ready to compare the benefits and concerns of a mentoring partnership?   Yes   No

7. Do the benefits outweigh the concerns?   Yes   No

8. Are you ready to take full advantage of a mentoring relationship?   Yes   No

Discussion:

In a small group of six to eight people, please discuss the following questions and share the highlights of your discussion with the whole group.

1. What do you see as the benefits of a mentoring partnership?

_____

_____

_____

2. What are you concerns about a mentoring partnership?

_____

_____

_____

Mentoring Partnership Agreement

Why establish a written agreement for a mentoring partnership? The Mentoring Partnership Agreement incorporates each partner's identified learning goals, agreed on learning outcomes, and the means for accomplishment. It reflects your conversation(s) regarding strategy and a work plan for creating a successful and satisfying mentoring relationship.

Mentoring Partnership Components:

1. Goals: State goals clearly and succinctly. They should be specific, action-oriented, realistic, and timely. What is to be learned and by whom?

    Mentor Partner (name):

    _____
    _____
    _____

    Mentor Partner (name):

    _____
    _____
    _____

2. **Success Criteria and Measurement:** Indicate how you will know you have achieved your stated goals. Describe the process, method, and milestones for evaluating success. Take into account that some adjustments and revisions may need to be made to keep the relationship focused and on track.

    Mentor Partner (name):

    _____
    _____
    _____

    Mentor Partner (name):

    _____
    _____
    _____

3. **Mentor Partnership Work Plan:** Describe your strategy for achieving mentoring partnership goals, including objectives and steps for completion (at minimum, the first few steps), learning/sharing opportunities, and a target date.

Mentor Partner (name):

_____

_____

_____

Mentor Partner (name):

_____

_____

_____

4. **Ground Rules:** List the practices and activities you have agreed to put in place in order to manage the partnership effectively and efficiently. Items to consider include meeting schedule, communication methods and styles, meeting agendas, and so on.

_____

_____

5. **Consensual Mentoring Agreement:** Additional information not included in the above listed items, for example, anticipated stumbling blocks, "what-if" situations and how they would be handled or dealt with, and other possible concerns relevant to a successful partnership. Remember to celebrate your successes.

_____

_____

_____

| Mentor Partner (name) | Signature | Date |

| Mentor Partner (name) | Signature | Date |

Orientation Part II: Initiating the Partnership
Evaluation

Thank you for participating in part II of the orientation, initiating the partnership, of your organization's Mentoring Partnership Program. In order for us to provide the very best experience, we are committed to continuous improvement and this can only be accomplished with your feedback. Please complete the following brief survey.

Please rate the following responses from 1 (not at all effective), 2 (somewhat effective), 3 (neutral), 4 (effective), to 5 (very effective); include a brief explanation.

1. How effective was the transition from part I of the orientation to part II? _____
    _____

2. How useful was the Are You Ready for a Mentoring Relationship? exercise? _____
    _____

3. Did working with other partnership teams help to effectively begin building a community? _____
    _____

4. How useful was the overview of the Mentoring Partner's Workbook? _____
    _____

5. How effective was the overview and discussion of the Mentoring Partnership Agreement? _____
    _____

Please briefly answer the following questions.

1. What went well?
    _____
    _____
    _____

2. How can the Initiating the Partnership session be improved?

_____

_____

_____

Additional comments:

_____

_____

_____

Chapter 4

Launch Meeting: Formalizing the Partnership

The official start of the mentoring program occurs at the second meeting—the launch meeting—where the partnership pairs or teams are brought back as a cohort to have the opportunity to become better acquainted with each other and begin bonding as a group.

Discussion topics for the launch meeting include the Mentoring Partnership Agreement, mentoring partnership meetings, feedback tips, accountability, and general discussions about communication, learning styles, and generational preferences.

Mentoring Partnership Agreement

Prior to this meeting, the matched partners have connected, as agreed to during the Initiating the Partnership meeting, to review and complete the partnership agreement form. This form provides a structured opportunity for the partners to reaffirm their compatibility and expectations for the relationship. A lengthy discussion should have taken place regarding:

- determining individual goals for the partnership, how these goals will be achieved, and indicators for success

- deciding learning matters and learning content

- scheduling the frequency of meetings, communication between meetings, and how the meetings will take place (for example, in-person, Skype, phone)

- addressing other items listed in the agreement form and as needed.

A completed and signed Mentoring Partnership Agreement should be submitted to the coordinator, formalizing the establishment of the partnership and a commitment to a six-month rotation. During the launch meeting participants share their experiences completing the form and provide feedback to the coordinator for improving content and format.

Mentoring Partnership Meetings

The launch meeting begins with exploratory conversations for developing a better understanding of the dynamics and clarifying the specifics of a mentoring relationship. Presentations and group discussions are conducted regarding the tools and tips for productive and empowering partnerships. These areas include the ground rules, work and communication styles, individual expectations, learning and development goals, and views on mentoring. Partners also need to be aware that as the relationship grows and expands, it may become necessary to change or amend some of the agreement items. The coordinator needs to assure the group that this is acceptable as long a revised, signed agreement is submitted for the file.

Strategies for Effective and Efficient Meetings

The Partner's Workbook includes productive mentoring strategies to use as a blueprint for utilizing individual skills and abilities in mentoring meetings. These complement each other and work well together to create a space where relationships can blossom and goals are reached.

Successful partnerships are fostered when:

- Confidence is built: Confidence is an essential factor in developing a professional and working relationship. It is a fundamental characteristic for coming together to complete agreed upon learning objectives and the means for accomplishment.

- Mistakes and errors are admitted: Taking responsibility for a slip-up or misunderstanding regarding actions or words and making necessary changes, clarifications, or corrections is vital for the partnership to move forward toward positive outcomes.

- Contributions to the partnership are acknowledged: A successful collaboration occurs when partners express appreciation to each other for upholding their part of the agreement and helping them to grow and develop.

- Time is used competently and responsibly: During a mentoring meeting people are focused on the matter at hand, prepared for the session, keep to the agenda, and turn off all communication devices (unless using one to hold the meeting).

- Partners come to their meetings with constructive mindsets: An open mind, positive views, and flexible attitudes enhance the relationship and bond.

Mentoring Partners' Feedback Tips

Receiving and giving feedback is often uncomfortable, but very important to effective learning and growth. Feedback should be a natural activity in a working relationship and is essential to increasing trust, productivity, strength, success, and a long-term perspective.

Helpful tips include:

- Ask for feedback: Be proactive, request specific and descriptive information. Indicate that both pro and con feedback is desired, because it is another way to learn.

- Be open to feedback: View it as a positive exchange, as a resource for improving both yourself and the relationship. Listen actively, be focused to really hear the feedback, and do not become defensive or take it personally. Ask for clarification, if necessary, and restate the feedback to make sure you heard it in the way it was meant. Then, acknowledge and thank your partner for the information and opinions.

- Accept the feedback: Reflect on what was said—how constructive was it, what surprised you, what challenged your self-image, and what impact could it have on your personal and professional development. Share any insights and reactions with your partner.

- Apply the feedback: Focus on your goals and priorities, and move forward by creating or revising an action plan that is specific, detailed, objective, and realistic. Periodically evaluate your progress, revise the plan accordingly to move forward, and ask your partner to review it for a second perspective.

- Give feedback: When providing observations and opinions, whether on request or spontaneously, it should be truthful, sincere, clearly communicated, relevant, and constructive. Set the context; be specific, straightforward, objective, and respectful of differences. Start with the positives and strengths before discussing weaknesses and errors. Think about how you will phrase your remarks and give feedback as you would like to receive it.

Think of feedback as a key strategy for keeping the partnership healthy, preventing miscommunications and misunderstandings, moving forward, and most important, not becoming dysfunctional.

Mentoring Partnership Accountability

An important component of a successful partnership is accountability to oneself, each other, and the program.

An accountability checklist is a useful tool to ensure that mentoring partnership meetings are on track and progress is being made toward goals. The partners are encouraged to complete this checklist as often as it is believed a review is necessary. Accountability elements include:

- holding regularly scheduled meetings

- coming prepared to meetings, with any assignments completed

- immediately clearing up any miscommunications or confusions

- checking in to be sure partners are on track with learning goals

- giving regular, two-way feedback

- resolving conflicts if they arise.

Communication, Learning Styles, and Generational Preferences

An important criterion to building a successful Mentoring Partnership team rapport is knowing the communication and learning styles of each partner. Because many, if not most, of the partnerships will be between individuals of different generations, another factor is an appreciation of the similarities and differences between each generations. During the launch meeting, partners will participate in small group activities intended to help them understand their own and others communication and learning styles, as well as an awareness of each generation's characteristics.

The primary purpose of a mentoring partnership is to foster learning and growth in personal and professional development. Understanding and acknowledging how we each communicate and learn is critical to the success of any mentoring partnership relationship.

Mentoring Partnership Communications

Communication between partners needs to be open and reflective and based on four basic characteristics that enable a strong relationship to be established, developed, and maintained: Shared Meaning, Authenticity, Respect, and Trust (SMART).

- Shared Meaning: It is the responsibility of both partners to clarify meanings, particularly at the beginning of the relationship. If participants know each other prior to this program, assumptions should not be made that they "really know" what the other person is saying. They should establish an environment of openness that welcomes questions, explanations, and acceptance.

- Authenticity: Genuine relationships are built on a commitment to communicate sincerely and honestly. Partners cannot hide behind a mask, but should always be their bona fide selves for confidence in the relationship to develop.

- Respect: Approach the partnership with mutual dignity, value, and appreciation. Partners may not always agree with each other, but should always feel that their ideas or opinions are respected. Respect is also particularly important when communication styles and preferences are different.

- Trust: This characteristic is the foundation for all communications between mentor partners and for a successful collaboration. People enter into a mentoring partnership assuming good intentions exist; however, trust grows over time as partners get to know each other, develop a certain level of closeness, and begin to feel comfortable in the relationship.

In addition, other important elements include:

- Active listening: It is not enough to hear; one also needs to actively listen to both the literal and the implied meanings of the words and message. Both verbal and nonverbal communication should be in sync showing genuine interest and sincere attention. It involves forgoing all other activities for the present and focusing on what is being said. Partners should be able to paraphrase each other's comments and concerns.

- Working communication plan: Set a schedule for how meetings are to be conducted. How will you communicate: in person, by phone, or by technological means? What factors or circumstances will determine which option will be chosen (for example, one partner or both on travel, busy schedules, combining business with a meal, and so on)? Consideration should be given to alternating different communication options to meet both partners' communication and working styles.

- Satisfaction level: Both partners should have a feeling of accomplishment at the conclusion of a mentoring meeting. If one or both of the partners does not believe that a session has been beneficial, this needs to be expressed and discussed before they part ways. Otherwise, a collaborative mentorship will not develop and trust will not grow.

Learning Styles

A critical component of the learning process is acknowledging and understanding our preference for how we learn. Several different models provide insights into how we learn and two of the most popular are Neil Fleming's VARK model and David Kolb's model based on experiential learning theory. Malcolm Knowles has also addressed adult learning theory.

Knowles's adult learning theory addresses the differences between how adults and children learn. These learning styles include:

- Problem-centered learning, which is focused on applied solutions rather than content.

- Results-oriented learning, which must lead to an outcome that is relevant to learner goals.

- Self-directed learning, which is when adult learners are involved in the development of a learning and outcomes evaluation.

- Experience-acknowledged learning, which is when the life experience of adult learners is acknowledged as a foundation for learning.

Fleming's VARK model includes the following terms or descriptions of learning styles:

- The visual learner, who thinks in pictures and prefers visual aids such as PowerPoints, handouts, or diagrams.

- The auditory learner, who learns through listening or discussions.

- The reading/writing preference learner, who learns by reading and writing notes.

- The kinesthetic learner, who learns by doing, applying, or via a hands-on approach.

Kolb's model consists of four modes of learning that should all be engaged for a complete learning experience. The four modes are:

- Convergers, who are good at making practical applications of ideas and using deductive reasoning to solve problems.

- Divergers, who are creative and good at coming up with new ideas and seeing things from a different perspective.

- Assimilators, who are good at creating theoretical models by means of inductive reasoning.

- Accomodators, who actively engage and do things instead of reading about them.

If we have a better understanding of how we learn and can appreciate how our mentor partner learns, the process of learning can be far more effective and productive for both of the partners.

This is also an opportunity to try learning styles beyond what we are comfortable with. Where might you learn? Think beyond the traditional mode of meeting in person, for example, you may instead decide to make on-site visits to see technical systems or equipment, informational interviews, view recommended webinars, or teleconference courses or workshops.

Generational Preferences

There are currently four generations in the workplace and the community, the Traditionalists (1925–1945), the Baby Boomers (1946–1964), Gen X (1964–1976), and Millennials or Gen Y (1977–1994). Gen Z or Gen Next (1995–2010) will soon be joining the workplace, too. We span at least 75 years in experience and our various viewpoints color how we practice basic communication and learning styles.

- Traditionalists:

  » Communication: formal, letters, memos, reluctant to embrace technology changes, schedule face-to-face meetings.

  » Learning style: instructor-led classroom delivery.

- Baby Boomers:

  » Communication: telephone or cell phone, face-to-face meetings, more flexible.

  » Learning style: instructor-led workshops.

- Gen X:

  » Communication: employs technology, informal conversations, flexible.

  » Learning style: e-learning and asynchronous learning.

- Millennials or Gen Y:

  » Communication: tech-savvy, social media, collaborative.

  » Learning style: hands-on, just-in-time, immediate relevancy.

GENERATIONAL DIFFERENCES				
	Traditionalists	**Baby Boomers**	**Gen X**	**Millennials**
Ideals	• Respect authority • Conservative values • Conformity • Discipline • Formality • Structured environment with clear expectations	• Optimistic • Involved • Hard workers • Lifelong learners	• Skeptical • Fun • Informal • Self-reliant	• Realistic • Confident • Extreme fun • Social and networking • Structured environment with clear expectations
Information Gathering	• Traditional media • Newspaper, radio, and television • Face-to-face meetings	• Mix of venues • Newspapers and online • Telephone/cell phone and email • Prefers face-to-face meetings	• Internet/online • Mobile devices • IM and texting • Avoid unnecessary meetings	• Social media • Texting • Peer-to-peer networks
Learning Motivation	• Knowledge of history and context • Public recognition • Training relevant to organizational goals • Leadership opportunities	• Public and peer recognition • Training relevant to career goals • Training by invitation as a perk	• Training relevant to personal goals • Recognition from instructor • Mentoring opportunities	• Training as fast track to success • Structured assignments with tight deadlines • Networking opportunities
Delivery Methods	• Accustomed to classroom-based lectures • Dislike role plays and learning games; they fear feeling foolish	• Accustomed to lecture and/or workshops • Small group exercises • Discussion may elicit "safe" rather than honest answers	• Accustomed to e-learning • Experiential learning, such as role play activities • On-the-job training and self-study, which allows them to multitask	• Accustomed to e-learning; leveraging wikis, blogs, podcasts, and mobile applications • Hands-on learning and collaboration leveraging technology
Feedback	• Assume they are meeting objectives unless they receive contrary feedback	• Prefer well-documented feedback all at once	• Prefer regular feedback	• Prefer frequent, on-demand feedback

In conclusion, the development of a working relationship between two people, no matter the purpose, starts with getting to know each other and feeling comfortable being together. Expectations are brought to any relationship and in a mentoring partnership these expectations include being compatible, having trust, and exchanging and sharing knowledge, skills, and experiences.

The Launch Meeting Delivery Process

The purpose of this meeting is to bring the mentoring partnership teams together to finalize the Mentoring Partnership Agreement, as well as to discuss next steps and the support system. The meeting should be held within two weeks of the orientation. The partners are eager to get started with their mentoring experience and delaying that because of administrative details could put a damper on that enthusiasm.

Meeting Goals

- Formalize the Mentoring Partnership Agreement.

- Review Mentoring Basics 101 protocol and procedures.

- Develop a sense of community for shared experience and support.

- Provide tips for productive and enriching relationships.

- Check in with coordinator and begin establishing a rapport.

Handouts and Forms

The following handouts or forms are found at the end of this section (pages 56-61) and in the Partner's Workbook:

- How Do I Communicate? How Can I Expand My Communication Options? Exercise

- Support of Mentoring Partnership Tips

- Mentoring Partnership Accountability Checklist

- Mentoring Partnership Accountability Discussion

- Launch Meeting: Formalizing the Partnership Evaluation.

Pre-Meeting Preparation

- Arrange a meeting location.

- Send an email invitation to participants with attendance confirmation.

- Remind participants to bring workbooks.

Agenda

This meeting is 2 to 2.5 hours depending on the size of group.

10 minutes	Welcome and reintroductions:

- After welcoming remarks conduct an icebreaker (for example, ask partners to share the most unlikely thing about themselves).

30 minutes	Review of the overall program:

- the goals of the program

- time commitment: six months

- communications exercise: mentoring partnership teams should complete the communication exercise and share the results

- commitment to open communication

- commitment to reflection

- regular meetings.

20 minutes	Review of the Mentoring Partnership Agreement:

- Discussion and feedback about agreement: This can be done in small groups of two or three partnership teams or if group has more than 12 participants, then it is more effective to have one large group activity.

30 minutes	Review strategies for success/reinforcement:

- Review the support tips, accountability checklist, and discussion questions.

15 minutes	Q&A:

- Make closing remarks.

- Announce mid-meeting date, time, and location.

- Complete Launch Meeting: Formalizing the Partnership Evaluation.

How Do I Communicate?
How Can I Expand My Communication Options?
Communications Awareness Exercise

Context: To be used in mentoring orientation programs and other training activities related to the development of a greater awareness of the differences in communication styles, language, and tools used among the generations. The ability to exchange and acknowledge ideas, knowledge, support, and advice is essential for an effective and meaningful mentoring partnership.

Learning Objectives:
- To increase understanding, acceptance, and recognition that various communication options exist.
- To increase cognizance that two people need to be "on the same wavelength" in order for mentoring to become a two-way, collaborative relationship.

Instructions:
1. Participants form small groups across the generations to discuss the ways they communicate most frequently and comfortably.

2. Each group is provided with paper and identifies a recorder/reporter. Take 15 to 20 minutes to discuss the following points of reference/topics.

   a. What are the two types of communication you use most frequently and why?

   b. What do you think of the types of communication that other people use?

   c. How do you think attitudes and mindsets about different types of communication can affect a mentoring partnership relationship?

   d. What do you think can be done to improve and expand communication options to increase the chances for a mentoring partnership to succeed?

3. Recorder/reporter gives a brief summary of the outcomes of the discussion to the group at large.

Support of Mentoring Partnership Tips

A primary benefit of the mentoring partnership is the concept of mutual learning and mutual support for that learning. Support means being there through the victories and the questioning, through growth and stalemates, through today and tomorrow. Here are a few tips for how we show support.

- Provide continual encouragement to help each other with positive reinforcement. A word or two of praise goes a long way toward self-confidence and stronger motivation to continue toward goals.

- Be an active listener and provide practical and constructive two-way feedback.

- Establish a mutual support system. Meetings held in a cooperative, assuring environment sustain the working relationship between the mentor partners.

- Encourage each other. A key element of creating an environment of growth is to believe that your partner is able to accomplish his or her goals.

Mentoring Partnership Accountability
Checklist

An accountability checklist is useful to assure that Mentoring Partnership meetings are on track and that progress is being made toward goals. Complete this checklist as often as a review is needed. Rate meetings against the following standards:

Standards	Always	Sometimes	Rarely	Never
Regularly scheduled meetings are held.				
We notify each other about schedule changes that can affect meetings.				
We come prepared to meetings and any assignments are completed.				
External distractions are removed during our meetings.				
Miscommunications and/or confusions are immediately cleared up.				
Assumptions are checked out.				
Check-ins are done to be sure we are on track with our learning goals.				
Feedback is conducted regularly and is two-way.				
Meetings are focused and productive.				
If conflict arises, we can resolve it.				

Mentoring Partnership Accountability Discussion

After partners complete and exchange session checklists, a discussion is scheduled regarding their compatibility and similar perceptions. (We recommend scheduling the discussion at the next session.)

Suggested questions for conversations include:

- Are both partners satisfied with the results? If yes, why? If no, why not and how will the differences be resolved or compromises be made?

- What can we do to improve the quality and results of our sessions?

- How would we describe how our relationship has been developing?

- Do we need to review and revise/update our agreement? If yes, is there any agreement about the specific changes and completion deadline?

- Are there any concerns or questions we would like to discuss with the coordinator?

Launch Meeting: Formalizing the Partnership
Evaluation

Thank you for participating in the launch meeting for formalizing the partnership of your organization's Mentoring Partnership Program. In order for us to provide the very best experience, we are committed to continuous improvement and this can only be accomplished with your feedback. Please complete the following brief survey.

Please rate the following responses from 1 (not at all effective), 2 (somewhat effective), 3 (neutral), 4 (effective), to 5 (very effective); include a brief explanation.

1. How useful is the Mentoring Partnership Agreement to you? _____

_____

2. How useful was the communications exercise? _____

_____

3. How effective were the meeting strategies and tips? _____

_____

4. How effective was the overall launch meeting? _____

_____

Please briefly answer the following questions.

1. What went well?

_____

_____

_____

2. How can it be improved?

_____

_____

_____

Additional comments:

_____

_____

_____

Chapter 5

Mid-Point Meeting: Checking In

The mid-point meeting is held approximately three months after the launch meeting and brings the individual Mentoring Partnership teams together. This gives everyone a way to reconnect with the other members of the cohort.

Mid-Point Meeting Delivery Process
Meeting Goals

- Provide partners with the support often needed to sustain the initiative.

- Continue the bonding and building of a community among the Mentoring Partnership teams.

- Get face-to-face contact with the coordinator and sustain the relationship.

- Allow participants to ask questions, compare their experience with the other teams, and confirm and recommit to their experience.

- Conduct a mid-point program evaluation and partnership relationship assessment.

- Encourage the completion and return of the individual self-reflection assessment.

Handouts and Forms

The following handouts or forms are found at the end of this section (pages 67-70) and in the Partner's Workbook:

- Individual Self-Reflections

- Mid-Point Partnership Experience: Reflections Exercise

- Mid-Point Meeting: Checking In Evaluation.

Preparation

- Arrange location for meeting.

- Send invitation to participants with program and partnership interim assessment forms to be completed and returned to coordinator or brought to meeting.

- Send follow-up invitations with additional reminders.

- Ask each mentoring partnership team to write a brief summary of their goals prior to the meeting to present at the meeting.

- Prepare copies of all handouts and forms in the event they are needed.

Note: If the meeting takes place in the evening, it is recommended that you provide light refreshments for a welcoming and supportive environment. However, if this is not possible, encourage participants to bring their own food.

Agenda

This meeting requires 2.5 hours.

10 minutes	Welcome and reintroductions:

- Ask participants to share any personal or professional updates.

20 minutes	Review of partnership goals:

- Teams summarize the goals stated in their agreement.

10 minutes	Mid-point program review:

- Restate that this information will be used to determine how the program is going and if adjustments need to be made at present.

- Ask participants, if comfortable, to share a summary of their feedback from submitted program assessments.

- Coordinator may want to comment on feedback received.

15 minutes	Mid-point partnership reflections:

- Participants complete the Mid-Point Partnership Experience: Reflection exercise.

- Restate that this information is a milestone indicator providing the coordinator with the status or potential success of individual partnerships.

- Ask participants, if comfortable, to share a summary of their comments from the submitted partnership assessments.

- Coordinator may want to comment on his perspective of the status of the partnerships.

15 minutes	Mid-point review of individual progress:

- Ask partners, if they are comfortable, to share their feelings about the mentoring partnership experience.

- Ask partners to share their individual progress as of today in accomplishing their goals.

5 minutes	Break

50 minutes	Networking:

- Exchange experiences and establish group support.

Discussion questions: Choose from among the following

or develop your own questions.

- How difficult was it to identify the agreement goals or operations of the partnership?

- Have there been changes to the goals or operations?

- How did you handle the changes?

- What have been the ways you have held your meetings?

- If any misunderstandings or miscommunications have occurred, how have they been resolved?

- What do you think is the best thing or benefit about your mentoring partnership?

10 minutes	Closing remarks:

- Review discussion highlights.

- Complete the Mid-Point Meeting: Checking In Evaluation.

- Announcement of celebration and final evaluations meeting date info.

Individual Self-Reflections
Mid-Point: Checking In

The purpose of the following questions is to give us a sense of where you are in your self-development so far and to give you an opportunity to reflect on how things are progressing. Please complete and return via email to _____ (name) by _____ (date).

1. What have you learned about yourself so far?

   _____

   _____

2. What have you learned from being part of a mentoring partnership?

   _____

   _____

3. Have your original goals evolved or changed?

   _____

   _____

4. How are you progressing in achieving your goals?

   _____

   _____

5. What experiences have gone well for you? Please explain.

   _____

   _____

6. What could be improved for you and how?

   _____

   _____

Mid-Point Partnership Experience
Reflections Exercise

The purpose of the following questions is to give us a sense of where you are in your partnership and to give you an opportunity to reflect on how things are progressing. Please be brief but thorough in your answers. This information will not go any further unless you wish to share. We hope you are having a wonderful experience.

1. Please rate on a scale from 1 (not at all effective), 2 (somewhat effective), 3 (neutral), 4 (effective), to 5 (very effective) how your mentoring partnership is progressing; include brief explanation. _____

   _____

2. How many times have you met? When did you have your first meeting?

   _____

   _____

3. Where or in what modes are you meeting (in person, via email, etc.)?

   _____

   _____

4. How are you progressing toward achieving your identified goal? Has your original goal(s) changed? Please explain.

   _____

   _____

5. Please rate how your partnership is developing; include a brief explanation.

   Not Working   Okay   Good   Great

   _____

   _____

Additional comments:

   _____

   _____

Mid-Point Meeting: Checking In
Evaluation

Thank you for participating in the mid-point meeting of your organization's Mentoring Partnership Program. In order for us to provide the best experience we are committed to continuous improvement and this can only be accomplished with your feedback. Please complete the following brief survey.

Please rate the following questions from 1 (not at all effective), 2 (somewhat effective), 3 (neutral), 4 (effective), to 5 (very effective); include brief explanation.

1. How effective are the partnership meetings? _____

_____

2. How effective is the mentoring partnership in progressing toward your goals? _____

_____

3. How effective is the Mentoring Partnership Agreement in keeping you on track? _____

_____

Please rate the importance of the following statements: 1 (not at all important), 2 (somewhat important), 3 (neutral), 4 (important), to 5 (very important).

1. How important is building the relationship of a partnership team? _____

_____

2. How important was it to be a part of the Mentoring Partnership Program cohort? _____

_____

3. Overall how would rate the value of the mid-point checking in meeting? _____

_____

4. How would you rate your experience so far? _____

_____

Please briefly answer the following questions.

1. How many times have you met since the launch meeting?

   _____

   _____

2. What have you learned?

   _____

   _____

3. Have you changed or revised your learning goals?

   _____

   _____

4. What are the changes or revisions?

   _____

   _____

5. What went well?

   _____

   _____

6. How can it be improved?

   _____

   _____

Additional comments:

_____

_____

_____

Chapter 6

Planned Celebration
and Closure Meeting

At the end of the Mentoring Partnership Program's six-month rotation, when the teams have accomplished their teaching and learning goals, it is important to plan a celebration for everyone that was involved. It also serves as formal closure and as an opportunity for a final review of the program and the developed partnerships. The event can be as small or large as you and the participants choose and budget allows. In addition to the Mentoring Partnership teams, the coordinator can also send invitations to the program staff members, representatives from senior leadership/board members, or participants' guests.

Closure Meeting Delivery Process
Meeting Goals

- To provide a way to officially bring closure to the six-month mentoring rotation.

- To acknowledge and congratulate the participants for a successful mentoring partnership and accomplishing their goals.

- To share perspectives and feedback regarding the program and mentoring model both orally and in a written evaluation form.

Materials, Handouts, and Forms

The facilitator should have the following materials:

- invitations

- handouts and forms

- participation/recognition certificates

- small appreciation gifts (if budget allows)

- sign-in sheets and name tags

- agenda.

The following handouts or forms are found at the end of this section (pages 75-78) and in the Partner's Workbook:

- Final Individual Self-Reflections

- Mentoring Partnership Experience: Final Reflections Exercise

- Closure Meeting: Final Overall Evaluation.

Pre-Meeting Preparation

Three to four months prior to the event:

- Arrange logistics: Schedule date and meeting location. The location will depend on whether the event will be a dinner or a reception.

- Note: If possible announce logistical arrangements at the mid-point meeting.

Four to six weeks prior to the event:

- Determine attendees: The coordinator will need to identify if any other guests will be invited other than the mentoring partnership teams.

- Prepare invitations: The invitations need to be designed, printed, and sent out with a RSVP deadline of one week before the event.

One month prior to the event:

- Prepare certificates: The Participation/Recognition Certificates need to be designed and printed.

- Create event program: The event program needs to be designed and printed.

Two weeks prior to the event:

- Send reminders: Email reminders to people who have not yet responded.

- Prepare evaluation forms: The final evaluation forms for individuals, partnerships, and program need to be printed.

- Buy small gifts: If planned and part of the budget.

One week prior to the event:

- Prepare handouts: Make sure all handouts are printed and ready to bring to the event.

- Confirm any catering orders.

Agenda

Two hours are required for this meeting.

10 minutes	Registration and pick up name tags.
10 minutes	Welcome and introductions.
30 minutes	Dinner, if this option is selected, otherwise move directly to the next agenda item.
20 minutes	Review of overall program: • Encourage participants to share their comments.
10 minutes	Break
25 minutes	Review of partnership and individual experiences: • Encourage participants to share their experiences.
15 minutes	Recognition of mentoring partnership teams and closing remarks.
30 minutes	Reception (if this option is selected it will end the event).

Final Individual Self-Reflections

The purpose of the following questions is to provide us with the final outcomes for your self-development as a participant in the Mentoring Partnership Program and to give you an opportunity to reflect on the results and next steps for your ongoing development.

1. What have you learned about yourself by participating in this program?

   _____

   _____

2. Overall, what have you learned from this mentoring partnership experience?

   _____

   _____

3. To what degree did you achieve your goals? 100%   75%   50%   25%   0%   Please explain.

   _____

   _____

4. What was the most important thing you learned from this experience?

   _____

   _____

5. What experiences went well for you? Please explain.

   _____

   _____

6. What could have gone better for you and how?

   _____

   _____

Mentoring Partnership Experience
Final Reflections Exercise

The purpose of the following questions is to give us a sense of your partnership and to give you an opportunity to reflect on your experience. Please be brief but thorough in your answers. This information will not go any further unless you choose to share. We hope you had a wonderful experience.

1. Please rate on a scale from 1 (not at all effective), 2 (somewhat effective), 3 (neutral), 4 (effective), to 5 (very effective) how your mentoring partnership progressed overall; include a brief explanation. _____

   _____

2. How many times did you meet in total? _____

3. Where or in what modes did you meet (in person, via email, etc.)?

   _____

4. Were your original goals achieved?   Yes   No

   If there were any revisions please describe them.

   _____

   _____

5. Were the revised goals achieved?   Yes   No

   Please explain.

   _____

   _____

6. Please rate how your partnership developed over time.

   Not Working   Okay   Good   Great

Additional comments:

_____

_____

Closure Meeting
Final Overall Evaluation

Thank you for participating in your organization's Mentoring Partnership Program. In order for us to provide the best experience, we are committed to continuous improvement and this can only be accomplished with your feedback. Please complete the following brief survey.

Please rate the following responses from 1 (not at all effective), 2 (somewhat effective), 3 (neutral), 4 (effective), to 5 (very effective); include brief explanation.

1. Overall, how effective was the mentoring partnership matching process?_____

_____

2. Overall, how effective was the Mentoring Partnership Agreement? _____

_____

3. Overall, how effective was your relationship with your mentoring partner? _____

_____

4. Overall, how effective was the mentoring partnership process in helping you accomplish your learning goals?_____

_____

5. How effective was the overall mentoring partnership experience?_____

_____

Please rate the importance of the following statement: 1 (not at all important), 2 (somewhat important), 3 (neutral), 4 (important), 5 (very important); include brief explanation.

1. Overall, how would you rate the value of the closing celebration? _____

_____

Please briefly answer the following questions.

1. What went well?

_____

_____

_____

2. How can it be improved?

_____

_____

_____

3. Would you recommend the Mentoring Partnership Program to a colleague? Please explain.

Yes   Maybe   No   Don't know

_____

_____

_____

Additional comments:

_____

_____

_____

Chapter 7

Program Administration

The Mentoring Partnership Program requires a formal structure led by a dedicated midlevel manager to direct the operation and cultivate the mentoring partnership team community. As with any new project, a proposal must be submitted and commitment gained from key stakeholders. If possible, a group meeting with identified stakeholders should be scheduled for a marketing presentation, to answer questions, and to ask for approval and support. The proposal writer then determines which decision makers need to review and authorize the mentoring partnership program.

Selection of Program Coordinator

The appointed coordinator can be a staff member who has other duties or a volunteer from the organization. Depending on the type of organization the coordinator will report to an HR staff member, a board member, or a senior-level executive. This person maybe the one who proposed the service or it may be another qualified person.

The role of the coordinator needs to be well defined and clearly understood by the selected staff member. One of the coordinator's most important qualifications must be a sincere belief in the value and benefits a mentoring program can bring to the organization and its employees. Consideration should also be given to the following questions: What are the qualifications to serve in this role? Will this position be housed in HRD, if not, where? What are the authority limits of the coordinator as far as setting program guidelines, policies, and participants' qualifications? How much independence does the coordinator have to resolve problems or issues?

Appointment of Team/Committee

The coordinator needs to select, at minimum, one person to assist in carrying out the responsibilities of the program. Depending on the envisioned size of the initial program, and other duties that the coordinator may have, a team or committee may be appointed. Team/committee members can be assigned clerical duties, for example, email blasts, tracking responses to emails and completed forms returned, scheduling meeting rooms, ordering refreshments, meeting registration duties, being on-call if coordinator is not available, and other duties as needed.

Coordinator's Management Responsibilities

In addition to planning program procedures, facilitating meetings, and organizing assessment activities as described in previous parts of this manual, the coordinator is also responsible for operational administration activities, including:

- Preparing and tracking the program budget. Line items include meeting supplies and refreshments, sets of participants' workbooks, promotional materials, meeting room rental fees, audiovisual equipment rentals, photo copying/printing, and so on.

- Liaising with senior-level executives to maintain support and involvement.

- Deciding the maximum number of partnerships that can be managed effectively and efficiently.

- Scheduling group meetings including room reservations, logistics, and preparations.

- Developing and conducting promotional and publicity materials for distribution using the organization's print, communication, and social media resources.

- Preparing progress reports, as required, both written and oral.

- Making recommendations for improvements, changes, and expansion, which will be submitted prior to the initiation of the next group of partnerships.

- Designing any additional forms, materials, or exercises needed for the organization and its members and culture.

Coordinator Engagement With Program Participants

The coordinator has a responsibility to develop and maintain open channels of communication with the program's participants. Encouraging candid dialogue and trust is critical for allowing difficulties to be expressed by one or both of the partners before irreparable damage is done to the working relationship. This is an important factor for the success of the program.

Consideration needs to be given to planned contacts, communication methods, and accessibility when a concern or question arises. Formal and informal channels need to be established for requesting updates of activities, learning how things are going, and asking if there are any problems or concerns. These communication activities should take place in addition to the meetings described previously and provide an opportunity for private one-on-one discussions. Thirty-minute bi-monthly conference calls should be scheduled between the coordinator and the mentoring partners. The coordinator should also be keeping in touch with partnership participants using email between each bi-monthly conference call.

The coordinator is also available to help with any questions or concerns that may arise between the planned points of contact and scheduled meetings. The coordinator should actively encourage staying in touch and stress that an "open door" policy exists starting from day one of the program.

Coordinator's Responsibilities to Retain Decision Makers' Commitment

The continual engagement of senior-level executives or board members is essential for the survival of the program and its budget. These decision makers need to see concrete evidence of the learning gained by participants and the added ROI value to the organization. Invite them to the launch, mid-point, and particularly, the celebration/closing meetings where they can interact with the participants and ask questions.

The coordinator may need to make changes or additions in operations, responsibilities, and so on to meet the individual organization's characteristics and culture. However, the partnership structure should remain the same due to the mentoring program's philosophy and premise, which is the core of this specific mentoring approach.

Evaluations and Final Report
Evaluation Targets

Evaluations should occur for four groupings: the individual, the partnership, the program, and the organization. Two evaluations are conducted during one six-month rotation—a mid-point assessment at the three-month mark and a final assessment at the end of the cycle.

- **Individual:** Evaluations at the individual level assess the status of achieving desired learning, experienced additional learning, received anticipated benefits in addition to learning, and overall satisfaction with the learning experience.

- **Partnership:** Evaluations at the partnership level track the quality of the sessions, the partnership relationship, and the progress toward goals by rating sessions and their characteristics against listed standards.

- **Program Operations/Management:** Evaluations at the program level focus on the overall administration and procedures, satisfaction with the coordinator's relationship with the partnership teams, and the extent of the community feeling within the mentoring cohort.

- **Organization:** Each organization designs its own individualized evaluation. It is recommended that this evaluation examine the ROI, the status of realizing expected benefits, and the development of a tracking system of past participants.

Final Report

An interim report can be submitted to the coordinator's immediate supervisor after the mid-point meeting. This summary is based on participant feedback in writing and verbally at the meeting.

The final report is critical as it includes recommendations for revisions, additions, and expansions to the program and is distributed to other senior-level executives beyond the immediate manager. This final report is not only based on summaries of the evaluations conducted as described above, but also a summary of the cohort meeting evaluations. The decision to continue to support the program is determined by the information and data presented.

Chapter 8

Promotional Activities

Promotional Initiatives

Publicity and recruitment activities should begin three months prior to the implementation of the mentoring partnership program. These various actions are to be treated as one whole and deliberately planned campaign to publicize this new service, including a logo, graphics, and overall design. Promotional materials ought to be easily recognized throughout the organization. Develop a list of all organizational communications and social media outlets. Also identify meetings where it would be appropriate to announce the program and distribute materials.

Communication Procedures: Recruitment

The first announcement to send out is a "Save the Date" for the orientation session. (See sample on page 87.) Next, a series of announcements should be sent out that provide meeting and contact information, as well as a registration form (with a deadline) to complete and return. (See samples of publicity pieces on pages 87-91.)

The Mentoring Partnership Program should also be promoted within the organization using:

- Newsletters: Write an article for newsletter, followed by short announcements.

- Email blasts: Send a minimum of four emails within the three months.

- Flyers: Post on bulletin boards, in cafeteria, lounges, the library, and so forth. Professional association chapters should have these flyers available at monthly meetings and networking events.

- Website: Post the announcement on the website's homepage. If the organization does not provide a blog page, then talk to the webmaster about one being initiated.

Communication Options for Future Participants

It is important to continue to publicize the program so that other people become aware of it and develop an interest in getting involved. By learning how their colleagues benefited from the program, they may be motivated to participate in a future mentoring partnership group. This type of communication can include:

- Newsletters: Include a follow-up report after the program launch, an article or two written by volunteer participants, or a descriptive report of the celebration and closing session in the company.

- Website: Post articles similar to the ones in the newsletter on the website.

- Blog/Open Journal: Have present and future partners, as well as the coordinator, use blogs and/or open journals to exchange and share their experiences, opinions, and ideas with each other and other members of the organization. This gives partners a space to reflect on how this experience is changing individuals. Blogging is a means for participants to identify with the program and become stakeholders in its growth and development.

Sample Save the Date

DATE

Mentoring Partnership Orientation Session

Are you interested in mentoring and being mentored? What about sharing your expertise and knowledge while at the same time gaining the benefit of someone's experience and skills? On **DATE** and **TIME** at **LOCATION,** we are initiating a Mentoring Partnership Program for staff and members with an orientation program facilitated by **NAME**. Please join us in this exciting project.

Further details coming soon. If interested, please email **EMAIL ADDRESS.**

Sample Flyer for Bulletin Boards or Meeting Handouts
COMPANY OR ORGANIZATION NAME

New Mentoring Partnership Program

Please join us in initiating this exciting benefit for **NAME!!**

First Group of Participants: January to June **(the program's six-month duration)**

Orientation Session: **DATE** and **TIME**

Are you interested in sharing your expertise and knowledge to give back to the chapter?

Would you like to benefit from someone else's skills and experiences?

The initial group will have a limited number of mentoring partners!

COMPANY OR ORGANIZATION is launching a Mentoring Partnership Program for employees and members. The first group will run from January to July, starting with an Orientation Session on **DATE**, from **TIME**, at **LOCATION**. **NAME** will introduce and coordinate this new service.

What is a Mentoring Partnership?

A mentoring partnership is a way to look at mentoring as a two-way inclusive interaction, with an exchange of ideas, knowledge, and expertise. There are learning benefits for both parties.

What will happen at the orientation session?

Participants will have an opportunity to exchange ideas and brainstorm about what they can offer and learn from a mentoring partnership. Small group discussions will follow about how different communication resources can be used to enhance and strengthen a mentoring relationship.

FACILITATOR NAME(S) will explain the mechanics and expectations of the program. We will provide a discussion guide and handouts about successful mentoring partnerships.

The orientation will end by establishing a limited number of partnerships. Please be aware that it may not be possible to match everyone in the first group.

About our facilitator(s):

INSERT INFORMATION HERE.

For further information and to RSVP by **DATE**, please email **EMAIL ADDRESS**.

Same Flyer for Bulletin Boards or Meeting Handouts
Mentoring Partnerships: A New Benefit for Members
Orientation Program

DATE and **TIME**

Facilitators: **NAMES**

Are you interested in mentoring someone to share your expertise and knowledge? Would you like to benefit from someone else's experiences, skills, and know-how? **COMPANY OR ORGANIZATION** is initiating a Mentoring Partnership Program for its members with a three-hour orientation program facilitated by **NAME**, who also gave us the presentation introducing the concept of mentoring partnerships at our **DATE** meeting.

Mentoring can be more than just effective and productive—it can be powerful, fluid, and energetic. In a traditional mentoring relationship, a senior-level person provides guidance, support, and information for a junior-level person, who is just beginning his or her life and career pathways. A mentoring partnership is different, because it is a two-way inclusive interaction, with an exchange of ideas, knowledge, and expertise, where generational status is not a factor. This collaboration or partnership provides learning benefits for both participants.

Orientation objectives:

- Introduce a partnership approach to mentoring whereby communications is considered to be a two-way interaction; generation status is not a factor; and learning, decision-making, and insights are benefits for both participants.

- Understand the various ways that communication in a mentoring relationship can take place and how different tools and styles can be used effectively.

- Initiate a Mentoring Partnership Program for the personal and professional development of its members by providing a matching process and procedure.

Program description: Participants will have an opportunity to exchange ideas and brainstorm about what they can contribute to, and want or need from, a mentoring partnership. Small group discussions will follow about how different communication tools and styles can be used to enhance and strengthen a mentoring partnership. **NAMES** will explain the mechanics and expectations of the Mentoring Partnership Program and a guide to a successful mentoring partnership will be distributed.

The orientation will end by establishing matched mentoring partnerships. Partners will complete an agreement of understanding regarding the shape and form of the partnership.

Please join us in initiating this exciting project for **COMPANY OR ORGANIZATION.**

About our facilitators:
INSERT INFORMATION HERE.

Sample E-Newsletter Announcement

COMPANY OR ORGANIZATION is launching a Mentoring Partnership Program for employees and members starting with an orientation meeting on **DATE** and **TIME** at **LOCATION** facilitated by **NAME(S)**, who will introduce and coordinate this new program.

A mentoring partnership is a way to look at mentoring as a two-way, inclusive exchange of ideas, knowledge, and expertise with mutual learning benefits for both participants. The orientation will conclude by establishing a limited number of partnerships. For further information and to RSVP by **DATE**, please email **EMAIL ADDRESS**.

Chapter 9

The Next Steps: Planning
for the Future

The six-month cycle for each cohort of mentoring partnership teams ends with a celebration and the submission of the final evaluation forms by the participants. Within the next month, the coordinator writes a final report, which is based on participant ratings and remarks as well as the coordinator's own experiences. This report is submitted to the supervisor and other relevant personnel. Senior executives may request oral presentations or a meeting to discuss ROI outcomes, the continuation of the program, and to recommended changes or revisions.

Sharing information and experiences is particularly important at the completion of the first mentorship cycle. The initial cohort can serve as program ambassadors and should be encouraged to promote the Mentor Partnership Model. They can explain this model and its benefits based on their own personal experiences. Everyone involved in the program—from senior executives to the participants—

should have had a learning experience, whether from successes or disappointments. If serious concerns or issues did develop during the first cohort, hopefully they were resolved before the end of the cycle.

Establish a Permanent Continuous Process

Planning for the next mentorship cohort should begin two months before the current cohort is finished. Because the current cohort hasn't finished, this will be before their evaluations have been completed and the final report and recommendations have been submitted. However, pre-planning and starting the new cycle is important to keep the program's momentum and buzz going. Any changes to the program based on feedback and evaluations from the current cohort can be made simultaneously with the planning of the next cohort.

The next orientation for the next cohort should be scheduled two months after the current cohort ends. Initiate an organized publicity campaign to increase awareness about the next round of mentoring partnerships by creating and distributing publicity materials announcing the date, time, and location of the next orientation meeting, as well as information about the program in general. These materials could include a "Save the Date" flyer, articles and quotes by participants, announcements on the organization's website or newsletter, and email blasts to relevant staff members.

Long-Term Perspective

Plan a longevity assessment to track the impact of operating a Mentoring Partnership Program on the organization and its ROI. Implementing a system to track the participants is important to determine whether the individuals and the organization/association are benefiting from the program. How have individual programs, services, and functions, for example, been changed, expanded, or initiated?

Three months after each rotation has ended, the cohort should complete a post-program review. A variety of tools can be used including an electronic feedback form, interviews of selected groups of participants, follow-up discussion sessions, or via feedback from participants' managers or board members regarding the impact they have observed regarding performance levels, involvement, or contributions made to the organization or association. At the end of each year, evidence of the long-term benefits and the value of the program can be noted.

This process must be completed with each new cohort to ensure that the program's ROI continues to be a positive asset.

The Future of Mentoring Partnership Programs

We plan to continue improving and expanding the model and updating its resources and tools. To meet our audience's needs and interests and to provide quality service, we invite your comments, input, and suggestions. Providing feedback about your experience with the Mentoring Partnership Program will help us to learn more about its strengths and discover its shortcomings. You can contact us at mentoringstrategies@gmail.com.

Part II

The Mentoring Partner's Workbook

Chapter 10

Introduction

Welcome to the Mentoring Partnership Program! You already learned about the differences between the Mentoring Partnership approach and the traditional mentor/protégé model. Now that you have begun to form your own mentoring partnership, you will discover that this program will help you and your partner to:

- Develop your skills and competencies for future career plans and professional capability.

- Explore future career directions and work options.

- Provide a sounding board to listen and to ask difficult questions.

- Share life experiences, specifically those dealing with new or difficult situations.

- Give support and encouragement to seek new challenges, to not become discouraged, and to persevere.

Which elements can you identify with for your mentoring experience?

Characteristics of an Effective Mentor

As a mentor, you are willing to commit to building productive and strong working relationships with your partner. Mentoring partners support the workplace values, mission, and goals. They bring their own unique organizational history and experience to a mentoring relationship.

Effective partners are able and willing to:

- Spend meaningful time in focused give and take discussions.

- Create a comfortable environment where they can be open and honest about views, feelings, and opinions.

- Share knowledge about the organization and its "way of doing things."

- Make introductions to people who can assist in achieving short-term professional and long-term career goals.

- Check periodically to ensure that expectations of both parties are in sync and realistic regarding the existing relationship.

- Allow feelings of frustration to be expressed and give candid and constructive feedback.

- Encourage testing new waters, trying-out different roles, and practicing new skills.

- Follow through on agreements made.

- Provide access to informal communication networks.

- Expand opportunities for visibility.

- Review career objectives and plans being developed for achievement and offer suggestions for improvement.

- Reinforce "lessons learned" when failure occurs and that risk is OK.

- Celebrate achievements and successes.

Having successfully participated in a self-selecting partnership match, it is expected that you will be able and willing to be:

- enthusiastic about another's dreams and aspirations

- motivating and encouraging about any new challenges, changes, or difficulties your partner may be facing

- open to sharing your experience with your partner about similar concerns, issues, or encounters

- empathic toward another's feelings, ideas, or outlook

- supportive toward the other's needs and concerns

- objective regarding the other person's solutions and action plans.

Productive mentoring results in experiences that are quite rewarding, educational, enriching, and appreciated by both parties.

The Mentoring Partnership Approach

The Mentoring Partnership Model is distinctive because it is intentionally designed and planned to build relationships that provide two-way inclusive interactions exchanging insights, knowledge, and expertise resulting in mutual learning benefits for both participants regardless of generational or workplace status. The diversity of our generations, cultures, and experiences bring many learning opportunities to the table.

This mentoring partnership is seen as a team assisting each other to improve and expand their strengths for themselves and their organizational success. This relationship involves a "give and take" style where people feel free and comfortable to express ideas and suggestions, ask for help, voice disagreements, and so on. A Mentoring Partnership team is an equitable association that connects two individuals bringing talents, skills, and experiences to the table that the other person wants to acquire.

Examples of learning that can occur include: passing on the organization's story, imparting technical skills, exchanging generational characteristics, advising how to fit into the organization's culture, and exchanging of job skills across departments.

Individual and Organization Benefits

Both participants involved in a Mentoring Partnership Program and the organization sponsoring the program benefit. Thus, it is a "win-win" situation enhancing both the individuals and the organization.

Individual benefits:

- Receive customized learning in a convenient one-on-one situation.

- Create new and stronger bonds among colleagues.

- Expand knowledge, insights, and expertise in organizational, personal, and professional arenas as a two-way learning exchange.

- Develop larger professional networks by having access to a new range of contacts made possible by a mentoring partner.

Organization benefits:

- Inspire new talent to identify with the organization and its culture by building stronger ties and working relationships.

- Retain the engagement of senior-level members with opportunities to learn while passing on their legacies.

- Sustain engagement and prevent loss of emerging talent.

- Enhance leadership and succession planning.

Guidelines and support resources are needed to establish and build an effective, successful mentor partnership and to develop a team mindset. This Workbook introduces the program and its activities. It also discusses recommendations and tips for developing a meaningful and productive working relationship. It is specifically designed to support participation in a mutual learning relationship.

Participating in a mentoring partnership program that provides the opportunity to build a sense of community with other partnerships enables you to enhance and expand your career, work opportunities, and networks, as well as your identity and commitment to your organization.

Chapter 11

Overview of Model Format

It is important for you and your partner to feel that you are not operating as a lone mentoring partnership, but are involved in an organizational program where people share concerns, experiences, and support. The process starts with an orientation meeting where mentoring partnerships are formed and closes with a celebration event where everyone can review their experiences, provide feedback, and reinforce their successes.

Orientation
Matching Process

The Mentoring Partnership Program begins with an orientation meeting for those who have expressed an interest in participating. The purpose is to introduce and discuss this mentoring approach, its goals, the six-month commitment, and the benefits of a self-matching mentoring partnership. Prior to the meeting you completed two forms, listing at least three things you wanted to learn and at least three things you were willing to teach or share in a two-way learning experience. The completed forms are brought to the first part of the orientation. The information you wrote on these forms is used to help you find your mentoring partner.

Initiating Partnerships

The initial matches have been made and this Workbook was distributed to those who were paired. The Workbook includes the Partnership Agreement, which is designed to help partner teams continue their conversations, make plans for future meetings, and become better acquainted. The initiating partnerships portion of the orientation is also an opportunity for the group to form a cohort designed to provide a community of support for all mentoring partnership teams.

Program Launch

The formal start of each program cycle begins about three weeks after orientation. Prior to the program launch meeting, partner teams should have connected to determine their compatibility and expectations for their relationship. The Partnership Agreement, which formally establishes the partnership and commitment to a six-month journey, should be completed, signed, and brought to the meeting.

Mid-Point Review

This meeting provides the mentoring partnership teams with a sense of community and support for their evolving journey. They can check in with other partnerships and compare their experiences and developing concerns/issues. This is also a good time to ask any questions that may have come up and give feedback as to how the program is going and if your partnership needs individual follow-up to strengthen its relationship.

Celebration and Evaluation

When the six-month journey is completed, a celebration is held to give everyone a sense of accomplishment and satisfaction, to recognize their achievements and the program's success. All participants have the opportunity to give feedback and suggestions for improvement. The leadership and coordinator will also share their views on the program's impact.

A formal email evaluation form will be sent to all participants to be completed, signed, and returned to the coordinator. Additionally, partners can decide to continue working together beyond this rotation.

Chapter 12

Mentoring Partnership Program Orientation

The orientation introduces the concepts and process of the Mentoring Partnership Model. In the first half, we presented an overview of the program and conducted the matching process for potential partners. The second half is the initializing or beginning of the partnership process. During this session partnership teams have the opportunity to get to know each other, receive the Workbook, and review the Partnership Agreement.

The Orientation Meeting
Meeting Goals

- Become better acquainted with your mentoring partner.

- Distribute and review the Partner's Workbook.

- Clarify the Partnership Agreement.

- Begin to develop mentoring partnership cohort community.

Agenda

- Review part I of the orientation meeting.

- Do the Are You Ready for a Mentoring Relationship? exercise.

- Go over the Workbook.

- Clarify and discuss the key role of Mentoring Partnership Agreement to the relationship's success.

- Have each partner team begin to review how they will complete the agreement.

- Discuss how partners will implement their mentoring partnership.

- Announce the launch meeting date.

- Complete the Orientation Part I: The Matching Process Evaluation and Orientation Part II: Initiating the Partnership Evaluation.

Orientation Part I: The Matching Process
Evaluation

Thank you for participating in the opening of your organization's Mentoring Partnership Program. In order for us to provide the very best experience, we are committed to continuous improvement and this can only be accomplished with your feedback. Please complete the following brief survey.

Please rate the following responses from 1 (not at all effective), 2 (somewhat effective), 3 (neutral), 4 (effective), to 5 (very effective); include a brief explanation.

1. How valuable was the promotion of the program? _____

    _____

2. Overall, how effective was part I of the orientation? _____

    _____

3. How effective were the teach and learn exercises for helping you identify your goals? _____

    _____

4. How effective was the process of posting and then reviewing other participants teach and learn aspirations? _____

    _____

5. How effective was the matching process? _____

    _____

Please briefly answer the following questions.

1. What went well?

    _____

    _____

    _____

2. How can it be improved?

_____

_____

_____

Additional comments:

_____

_____

_____

Are You Ready for a Mentoring Relationship?
Exercise

The purpose of this review is to help you determine if you are ready for a mentoring relationship. The questions will help you evaluate yourself and your motivation. Please circle the appropriate answer.

1. Do you believe a mentor would be of help to your growth at this time?   Yes   No

2. Are you willing to commit the time, energy, and resolve needed for a successful mentoring relationship?   Yes   No

3. Are you ready to learn, listen, and ask questions?   Yes   No

4. Are you willing to hear and accept feedback and to give equally productive feedback?   Yes   No

5. Are you ready to develop an open, honest, and transparent relationship committed to achieving the goals of a mentoring partnership?   Yes   No

6. Are you ready to compare the benefits and concerns of a mentoring partnership?   Yes   No

7. Do the benefits outweigh the concerns?   Yes   No

8. Are you ready to take full advantage of a mentoring relationship?   Yes   No

Discussion: In a small group of six to eight people, please discuss the following questions and share the highlights of your discussion with the whole group.

1. What do you see as the benefits of a mentoring relationship?

_____

_____

_____

_____

2. What are your concerns about a mentoring relationship?

_____

_____

_____

_____

Mentoring Partnership Agreement

Why establish a written agreement for a mentoring partnership? The Mentoring Partnership Agreement incorporates each partner's identified learning goals, agreed on learning outcomes, and the means for accomplishment. It reflects your conversation(s) regarding strategy and a work plan for creating a successful and satisfying mentoring relationship.

Mentoring Partnership Components:

1. **Goals:** State goals clearly and succinctly. They should be specific, action-oriented, realistic, and timely. What is to be learned and by whom?

   Mentor Partner (name):

   _____

   _____

   _____

   Mentor Partner (name):

   _____

   _____

   _____

2. **Success Criteria and Measurement:** Indicate how you will know you have achieved your stated goals. Describe the process, method, and milestones for evaluating success. Take into account that some adjustments and revisions may need to be made to keep the relationship focused and on track.

   Mentor Partner (name):

   _____

   _____

   _____

   Mentor Partner (name):

   _____

   _____

   _____

3. **Mentor Partnership Work Plan:** Describe your strategy for achieving mentoring partnership goals, including objectives and steps for completion (at minimum, the first few steps), learning/sharing opportunities, and a target date.

Mentor Partner (name):

_____

_____

Mentor Partner (name):

_____

_____

4. **Ground Rules:** List the practices and activities you have agreed to put into place in order to manage the partnership effectively and efficiently. Items to consider include meeting schedule, communication methods and styles, meeting agendas, and so on.

_____

_____

5. **Consensual Mentoring Agreement:** Additional information not included in the above listed items, for example, anticipated stumbling blocks, "what-if" situations and how they would be handled or dealt with, and other possible concerns relevant to a successful partnership. Remember to celebrate your successes.

_____

_____

_____

_____

Mentor Partner (name)	Signature	Date

Mentor Partner (name)	Signature	Date

Orientation Part II: Initiating the Partnership
Evaluation

Thank you for participating in part II of the orientation, initiating the partnership, of your organization's Mentoring Partnership Program. In order for us to provide the very best experience, we are committed to continuous improvement and this can only be accomplished with your feedback. Please complete the following brief survey.

Please rate the following responses from 1 (not at all effective), 2 (somewhat effective), 3 (neutral), 4 (effective), to 5 (very effective); include a brief explanation.

1. How effective was the transition from part I of the orientation to part II? _____

_____

2. How useful was the Are You Ready for a Mentoring Relationship? exercise? _____

_____

3. Did working with other partnership teams help to effectively begin building a community? _____

_____

4. How useful was the overview of the Mentoring Partner's Workbook? _____

_____

5. How effective was the overview and discussion of the Mentoring Partnership Agreement? _____

_____

Please briefly answer the following questions.

1. What went well?

_____

_____

2. How can the Initiating the Partnership session be improved?

_____

_____

_____

Additional comments:

_____

_____

_____

Chapter 13

Launch Meeting: Formalizing the Partnership

The official start of the actual mentoring program occurs at the second meeting—the launch meeting—where the partnership pairs or teams are brought back as a cohort to have the opportunity to become better acquainted with each other and begin bonding as a group.

Mentoring Partnership Agreement

Prior to this meeting, you and your partner have connected, as agreed during orientation, to review and complete the partnership agreement form, which provides a structure to determine your compatibility and expectations for the mentoring relationship. A lengthy discussion should have taken place regarding such topics as:

- defining individual goals for the partnership, how these goals will be achieved, and indicators determining success

- deciding how one learns matters and content

- determining the frequency of meetings, how to communicate between meetings, and how your meetings will take place (for example, in-person, Skype, phone)

- addressing other items listed in the agreement form and as needed.

The completed and signed Partnership Agreement should have been submitted to the coordinator, formalizing the establishment of the partnership and a commitment to a six-month rotation. During the launch meeting partners should share their experiences completing the form and provide feedback to the coordinator for improving the form's content and format.

Mentoring Partnership Meetings

The launch meeting begins with exploratory conversations for developing a better understanding of the dynamics and clarifying the specifics of a mentoring relationship. Presentations and group discussions are conducted regarding the tools and tips for productive and empowering partnerships. These areas include the ground rules, learning and communication styles, individual expectations, learning and development goals, and views on mentoring. Partners also need to be aware that as the relationship grows and expands, it may become necessary to change or amend some of the agreement items. The coordinator needs to assure the group that this is acceptable as long as you submit a revised, signed agreement to the coordinator.

Strategies for Effective and Efficient Meetings

Your Partner's Workbook includes productive mentoring strategies to use as a blueprint for utilizing individual skills and abilities in mentoring meetings. These strategies complement each other and create a space where relationships can blossom and goals are reached.

Successful partnerships are fostered when:

- Confidence is built: Confidence is an essential factor in developing a professional and working relationship. It is a fundamental characteristic for coming together to meet agreed upon learning objectives and the means for accomplishment.

- Mistakes and errors are admitted: Taking responsibility for a slip-up or misunderstanding regarding actions or words and making necessary changes, clarifications, or corrections is vital for allowing the partnership to move forward toward positive outcomes.

- Contributions to the partnership are acknowledged: A successful collaboration occurs when partners express their appreciation to each other for upholding their part of the agreement and helping them to grow and develop.

- Time is used competently and responsibly: During a mentoring meeting people are focused on the matter at hand, prepared for the session, keep to the agenda, and turn off all communication devices (unless using one to hold the meeting).

- Partners come to the meeting with constructive mindsets: An open mind, positive views, and flexible attitudes enhance the relationship and bond.

Mentoring Partners' Feedback Tips

Giving and receiving feedback is often uncomfortable, but it is also very important to effective learning and growth. Feedback should be a natural activity in a working relationship and is essential to increasing trust, productivity, strength, success, and a long-term perspective.

Helpful tips include:

- Ask for feedback: Be proactive. Request specific and descriptive information and indicate that both pro and con feedback is desired, because it is another way to learn and view.

- Be open to feedback: View it as a positive exchange, as a resource for improving both yourself and the relationship. Listen actively, be focused to really hear the feedback, and do not become defensive or take it personally. Ask for clarification, if necessary, and restate the feedback to make sure you heard it in the way it was meant. Then, acknowledge and thank your partner for the information and opinions.

- Accept the feedback: Reflect on what was said—how constructive was it, what surprised you, what challenged your self-image, and what impact could it have on your personal and professional development. Share any insights and reactions with your partner.

- Apply the feedback: Focus on your goals and priorities, and move forward by creating or revising an action plan that is specific, detailed, objective, and realistic. Periodically evaluate your progress, revise the plan accordingly to move forward, and ask your partner to review it for a second perspective.

- Give feedback: When providing observations and opinions, whether on request or spontaneously, it should be truthful, sincere, clearly communicated, relevant, and constructive. Set the context; be specific, straightforward, objective, and respectful of differences. Start with the positives and strengths before discussing weaknesses and errors. Think about how you will phrase your remarks and give feedback as you would like to receive it.

Think of feedback as a key strategy for keeping the partnership healthy, preventing miscommunications and misunderstandings, moving forward, and most important, not becoming dysfunctional.

Mentoring Partnership Accountability

An important component of a successful partnership is accountability to oneself, each other, and the program.

An accountability checklist is a useful tool to assure that mentoring partnership meetings are on track and progress is being made toward goals. Partners are encouraged to complete this checklist as often as it is believed a review is needed.

Accountability elements include:

- holding regularly scheduled meetings

- coming prepared to meetings, with any assignments completed

- immediately clearing up any miscommunications or confusions

- checking into be sure partners are on track with learning goals

- giving regular, two-way feedback

- resolving conflicts if they arise.

Communications, Learning Styles, and Generational Preferences

An important criterion to building a successful Mentoring Partnership team rapport is the knowing the communications and learning styles of each partner. Because you and your partner most likely will be of different generations, another factor to consider is an appreciation of the similarities and differences between the generations. During this meeting you will participate in small group activities intended to help you understand your own and others communication and learning styles, as well as an awareness of each generation's characteristics.

The primary purpose of a mentoring partnership is to foster learning and growth in personal and professional development. Understanding and acknowledging how we each communicate and learn is critical to the success of any mentoring partnership relationship.

Mentoring Partnership Communications

Communication between partners needs to be open and reflective and based on four basic characteristics that enable a strong relationship to be established, developed, and maintained: Shared Meaning, Authenticity, Respect, and Trust (SMART).

- Shared Meaning: It is the responsibility of both partners to clarify meanings, particularly at the beginning of the relationship. If you knew your partner before participating in this program, you should not make assumptions that you really "know" what your partner is saying. An environment of openness should be established that welcomes questions, explanations, and acceptance.

- Authenticity: Genuine relationships are built on a commitment to communicate sincerely and honestly. Partners cannot hide behind a mask, but should always be their bona fide selves for confidence in the relationship to develop.

- Respect: Approach the partnership with mutual dignity, value, and appreciation. Partners may not always agree with each other, but should always feel that their ideas or opinions are respected. Respect is also particularly important when communication styles and preferences are different.

- Trust: This characteristic is the foundation for all communications between mentor partners and for a successful collaboration. People enter into a mentoring partnership assuming good intentions exist; however, trust grows over time as partners get to know each other, develop a certain level of closeness, and begin to feel comfortable in the relationship.

In addition, other important elements include:

- Active listening: It is not enough to hear; one also needs to actively listen to both the literal and the implied meanings of the words and message. Both verbal and nonverbal communication should be in sync showing genuine interest and sincere attention. It involves forgoing all other activities for the present and focusing on what is being said. Partners should be able to paraphrase comments and concerns.

- Working communication plan: Set a schedule for how meetings are to be conducted. How will you communicate: in person, by phone, or by technological means? What factors or circumstances will determine which option will be chosen(for example, one partner or both on travel, busy schedules, combining business with a meal, and so on)?

Consideration should be given to alternating different communication options to meet both partners' communication and working styles.

- Satisfaction level: Both partners should have a feeling of accomplishment at the conclusion of a mentoring meeting. If one or both of the partners does not believe that a session has been beneficial, this needs to be expressed and discussed before they part ways. Otherwise, a collaborative mentorship will not develop and trust will not grow.

Learning Styles

A critical component of the learning process is acknowledging and understanding your preference for how you learn. Several different models provide insight into how we learn, two of the most popular are Neil Fleming's VARK model and David Kolb's model based on experiential learning theory. Malcolm Knowles has also addressed adult learning theory.

Knowles's adult learning theory addresses the differences between how adults and children learn. These learning styles include:

- Problem-centered learning, which is focused on applied solutions rather than content.

- Results-oriented learning, which must lead to an outcome that is relevant to learner goals.

- Self-directed learning, which is when adult learners are involved in the development of a learning and outcomes evaluation.

- Experience-acknowledged learning, which is when the life experience of adult learners is acknowledged as a foundation for learning.

Fleming's VARK model includes the following terms or descriptions of learning styles:

- The visual learner, who thinks in pictures and prefers visual aids such as PowerPoints, handouts, or diagrams.

- The auditory learner, who learns through listening or discussions.

- The reading/writing preference learner, who learns by reading and writing notes.

- The kinesthetic learner, who learns by doing, applying, or via a hands on approach.

Kolb's model consists of four modes of learning that should all be engaged for a complete learning experience. The four modes are:

- Convergers,who are good at making practical applications of ideas and using deductive reasoning to solve problems.

- Divergers, who are creative and good at coming up with new ideas and seeing things from a different perspective.

- Assimilators, who are good at creating theoretical models by means of inductive reasoning.

- Accomodators, who actively engage and do things instead of reading about them.

If you have a better understanding of how you learn and can appreciate how your mentoring partner learns, the process of learning can be far more effective and productive for both of you.

This is also an opportunity to try learning styles beyond what you are comfortable with. Where might you learn? Think beyond the traditional meeting, perhaps you could make on-site visits to see technical systems or equipment, informational interviews, view recommended webinars, or attend teleconference courses or workshops.

Generational Preferences

There are currently four generations in the workplace and the community, the Traditionalists (1925–1945), the Baby Boomers (1946–1964), Gen X (1964–1976), and the Millennials or Gen Y (1977–1994). Gen Z or Gen Next (1995–2010) will soon be joining the workplace, too. We span at least 75 years in experience and our various viewpoints color how we practice basic communication and learning styles.

- Traditionalists:

  - » Communication: formal, letters, memos, reluctant to embrace technology changes, and schedule face-to-face meetings.

  - » Learning style: instructor-led classroom delivery.

- Baby Boomers:

  - » Communication: telephone or cellphone, face-to-face meetings, and are more flexible.

  - » Learning style: instructor-led workshops.

- Gen X:

  - » Communication: employs technology, informal conversations, flexible and telecommuting.

  - » Learning style: e-learning and asynchronous learning.

- Millennials or Gen Y:

  - » Communication: tech-savvy, social media, collaborative.

  - » Learning style: hands-on, just-in-time, immediate relevancy.

GENERATIONAL DIFFERENCES			
Traditionalists	**Baby Boomers**	**Gen X**	**Millennials**
Ideals • Respect authority • Conservative values • Conformity • Discipline • Formality • Structured environment with clear expectations	• Optimistic • Involved • Hard workers • Lifelong learners	• Skeptical • Fun • Informal • Self-reliant	• Realistic • Confident • Extreme fun • Social and networking • Structured environment with clear expectations
Information Gathering • Traditional media • Newspaper, radio, and television • Face-to-face meetings	• Mix of venues • Newspapers and online • Telephone/cell phone and email • Prefers face-to-face meetings	• Internet/online • Mobile devices • IM and texting • Avoid unnecessary meetings	• Social media • Texting • Peer-to-peer networks
Learning Motivation • Knowledge of history and context • Public recognition • Training relevant to organizational goals • Leadership opportunities	• Public and peer recognition • Training relevant to career goals • Training by invitation as a perk	• Training relevant to personal goals • Recognition from instructor • Mentoring opportunities	• Training as fast track to success • Structured assignments with tight deadlines • Networking opportunities
Delivery Methods • Accustomed to classroom-based lectures • Dislike role plays and learning games; they fear feeling foolish	• Accustomed to lecture and/or workshops • Small group exercises • Discussion may elicit "safe" rather than honest answers	• Accustomed to e-learning • Experiential learning, such as role play activities • On-the-job training and self-study, which allows them to multitask	• Accustomed to e-learning; leveraging wikis, blogs, podcasts, and mobile applications • Hands-on learning and collaboration leveraging technology
Feedback • Assume they are meeting objectives unless they receive contrary feedback	• Prefer well-documented feedback all at once	• Prefer regular feedback	• Prefer frequent, on-demand feedback

In conclusion, the development of a working relationship between two people, no matter the purpose, starts with getting to know each other and feeling comfortable being together. Expectations are brought to any relationship and in a mentoring partnership these expectations include being compatible; developing trust; and exchanging and sharing knowledge, skills, and experiences.

The Launch Meeting

The purpose of this meeting is to bring the mentoring partnership teams together to finalize the Mentoring Partnership Agreement, as well as to discuss next steps and the support system. The meeting should be held within two weeks of part II of the orientation.

Meeting Goals

- Formalize the Mentoring Partnership Agreement.

- Review Mentoring Basics 101 protocol and procedures.

- Develop a sense of community for shared experience and support.

- Provide tips for productive and enriching relationships.

- Check in with coordinator and begin establishing a rapport.

Agenda

- Conduct welcome and reintroductions.

- Do the communications exercise.

- Review the overall program.

- Review the Mentoring Partnership Agreement.

- Review strategies for success/reinforcement.

- Go over any Q&A.

- Finish with closing remarks.

How Do I Communicate?

How Can I Expand My Communication Options?

Communications Awareness Exercise

Context: To be used in mentoring orientation programs and other training activities related to the development of a greater awareness of the differences in communication styles, language, and tools used among the generations. The ability to exchange and acknowledge ideas, knowledge, support, and advice is essential for an effective and meaningful mentoring partnership.

Learning Objectives:

- To increase understanding, acceptance, and recognition that various communication options exist.

- To increase cognizance that two people need to be "on the same wavelength" in order for mentoring to become a two-way, collaborative relationship.

Instructions:

1. Participants form small groups across the generations to discuss the ways they communicate most frequently and comfortably.

2. Each group is provided with paper and identifies a recorder/reporter. Take 15 to 20 minutes to discuss the following points of reference/topics.

    a. What are the two types of communication you use most frequently and why?

    b. What do you think of the types of communication that other people use?

    c. How do you think attitudes and mindsets about different types of communication can affect a mentoring partnership relationship?

    d. What do you think can be done to improve and expand communication options to increase the chances for a mentoring partnership to succeed?

3. Recorder/reporter gives a brief summary of the outcomes of the discussion to the group at large.

Support of Mentoring Partnership Tips

A primary benefit of the mentoring partnership is the concept of mutual learning and mutual support for that learning. Support means being there through the victories and the questioning, through growth and stalemates, through today and tomorrow. Here are a few tips for how we show support.

- Provide continual encouragement to help each with positive reinforcement. A word or two of praise goes a long way toward self-confidence and boosting motivation to continue toward goals.
- Be an active listener and provide practical and constructive two-way feedback.
- Establish a mutual support system. Meetings held in a cooperative, assuring environment sustain the working relationship between the mentor partners.
- Encourage each other. A key element of creating an environment of growth is to believe that your partner is able to accomplish his or her goals.

Mentoring Partnership Accountability
Checklist

An accountability checklist is useful to assure that Mentoring Partnership meetings are on track and that progress is being made toward goals. Complete this checklist as often a review is needed. Rate meetings against the following standards:

Standards	Always	Sometimes	Rarely	Never
Regularly scheduled meetings are held.				
We notify each other about schedule changes that can affect meetings.				
We come prepared to meetings and any assignments are completed.				
External distractions are removed during our meetings.				
Miscommunications and/or confusions are immediately cleared up.				
Assumptions are checked out.				
Check-ins are done to be sure we are on track with our learning goals.				
Feedback is conducted regularly and is two-way.				
Meetings are focused and productive.				
If conflict arises, we can resolve it.				

Mentoring Partnership Accountability Discussion

After partners complete and exchange session checklists, a discussion is scheduled regarding their compatibility and similar perceptions. (We recommend scheduling the discussion at the next session.)

Suggested questions for conversations include:

- Are both partners satisfied with the results? If yes, why? If no, why not and how will the differences be resolved or compromises be made?

- What can we do to improve the quality and results of our sessions?

- How would we describe how our relationship has been developing?

- Do we need to review and revise/update our agreement? If yes, is there any agreement about the specific changes and completion deadline?

- Are there any concerns or questions we would like to discuss with the coordinator?

Launch Meeting: Formalizing the Partnership
Evaluation

Thank you for participating in the launch meeting for formalizing the partnership of your organization's Mentoring Partnership Program. In order for us to provide the very best experience, we are committed to continuous improvement and this can only be accomplished with your feedback. Please complete the following brief survey.

Please rate the following responses from 1 (not at all effective), 2 (somewhat effective), 3 (neutral), 4 (effective), to 5 (very effective); include a brief explanation.

1. How useful is the Mentoring Partnership Agreement to you? _____

_____

2. How useful was the communications exercise? _____

_____

3. How effective were the meeting strategies and tips? _____

_____

4. How effective was the overall launch meeting? _____

_____

Please briefly answer the following questions.

1. What went well?

_____

_____

_____

2. How can it be improved?

_____

_____

_____

Additional comments:

_____

_____

_____

Chapter 14

Mid-Point Meeting: Checking In

The mid-point meeting is held approximately three months after the launch meeting and brings the individual Mentoring Partnership teams together. This gives everyone a way to reconnect with the other members of the cohort.

Mid-Point Meeting

Meeting Goals

- Provide partners with the support often needed to sustain the initiative.

- Continue the bonding and building of a community among the Mentoring Partnership teams.

- Get face-to-face contact with the coordinator and sustain the relationship.

- Allow participants to ask questions, compare their experience with the other teams, and confirm and recommit to their experience.

- Complete a mid-point program evaluation and partnership relationship assessment.

Agenda

- Conduct welcome and reintroductions.

- Review the partnership goals.

- Review the mid-point partnership reflections, individual self-reflections, and the evaluation.

- Network.

- Finish with closing remarks.

Individual Self-Reflections
Mid-Point: Checking In

The purpose of the following questions is to give us a sense of where you are in your self-development so far and to give you an opportunity to reflect on how things are progressing. Please complete and return via email to _____ (name) by _____ (date).

1. What have you learned about yourself so far?

   _____

   _____

2. What have you learned from being part of a mentoring partnership?

   _____

   _____

3. Have your original goals evolved or changed?

   _____

   _____

4. How are you progressing in achieving your goals?

   _____

   _____

5. What experiences have gone well for you? Please explain.

   _____

   _____

6. What could be improved for you and how?

   _____

   _____

Mid-Point Partnership Experience
Reflections Exercise

The purpose of the following questions is to give us a sense of where you are in your partnership and to give you an opportunity to reflect on how things are progressing. Please be brief but thorough in your answers. This information will not go any further unless you wish to share. We hope you are having a wonderful experience.

1. Please rate on a scale from 1 (not at all effective), 2 (somewhat effective), 3 (neutral), 4 (effective), to 5 (very effective) how your mentoring partnership is progressing; include brief explanation. _____

   _____

2. How many times have you met? When did you have your first meeting?

   _____

   _____

3. Where or in what modes are you meeting (in person, via email, etc.)?

   _____

   _____

4. How are you progressing toward achieving your identified goal? Has your original goal(s) changed? Please explain.

   _____

   _____

5. Please rate how your partnership is developing; include a brief explanation.
   Not Working   Okay   Good   Great

   _____

   _____

Additional comments:

   _____

   _____

   _____

Mid-Point Meeting: Checking In
Evaluation

Thank you for participating in the mid-point meeting of your organization's Mentoring Partnership Program. In order for us to provide the best experience we are committed to continuous improvement and this can only be accomplished with your feedback. Please complete the following brief survey.

Please rate the following questions from 1 (not at all effective), 2 (somewhat effective), 3 (neutral), 4 (effective), to 5 (very effective); include brief explanation.

1. How effective are the partnership meetings? _____

_____

2. How effective is the mentoring partnership in progressing toward your goals? _____

_____

3. How effective is the Mentoring Partnership Agreement in keeping you on track? _____

_____

Please rate the importance of the following statements: 1 (not at all important), 2 (somewhat important), 3 (neutral), 4 (important), to 5 (very important).

1. How important is building the relationship of a partnership team? _____

_____

2. How important was it to be a part of the Mentoring Partnership Program cohort? _____

_____

3. Overall how would rate the value of the mid-point checking in meeting? _____

_____

4. How would you rate your experience so far? _____

_____

Please briefly answer the following questions.

1. How many times have you met since the launch meeting?

_____

_____

2. What have you learned?

_____

_____

3. Have you changed or revised your learning goals?

_____

_____

4. What are the changes or revisions?

_____

_____

5. What went well?

_____

_____

6. How can it be improved?

_____

_____

Additional comments:

_____

_____

_____

Chapter 15

Planned Celebration
and Closure Meeting

At the end of the Mentoring Partnership Program's six-month rotation, when the teams have accomplished their teaching and learning goals, it is important to plan a celebration for everyone that was involved. This also serves as a formal closure and as an opportunity for a final review of the program and the developed partnerships.

Closure Meeting
Meeting Goals

- To provide a way to officially bring closure to the six-month mentoring rotation.

- To acknowledge and congratulate the participants for a successful mentoring partnership and accomplishing their goals.

- To share perspectives and feedback regarding the program and mentoring model both orally and in a written evaluation form.

Agenda

- Conduct welcome and introductions.

- Review the overall program.

- Review the partnership experiences.

- Recognize the mentoring partnership teams.

- Hold reception or dinner (optional).

- Finish with closing remarks.

Final Individual Self-Reflections

The purpose of the following questions is to provide us with the final outcomes for your self-development as a participant in the Mentoring Partnership Program and to give you an opportunity to reflect for yourself the results and next steps for your ongoing development.

1. What have you learned about yourself by participating in this program?

   _____

   _____

2. Overall, what have you learned from this mentoring partnership experience?

   _____

   _____

3. To what degree did you achieve your goals? 100% 75% 50% 25% 0% Please explain.

   _____

   _____

4. What was the most important thing you learned from this experience?

   _____

   _____

5. What experiences went well for you? Please explain.

   _____

   _____

6. What could have gone better for you and how?

   _____

   _____

Mentoring Partnership Experience
Final Reflections Exercise

The purpose of the following questions is to give us a sense of your partnership and to give you an opportunity to reflect on your experience. Please be brief but thorough in your answers. This information will not go any further unless you choose to share. We hope you had a wonderful experience.

1. Please rate on a scale from 1 (not at all effective), 2 (somewhat effective), 3 (neutral), 4 (effective), to 5 (very effective) how your mentoring partnership progressed overall; include a brief explanation. _____

   _____

2. How many times did you meet in total? _____

3. Where or in what modes did you meet (e.g., in person, via email, etc.)?

   _____

4. Were your original goals achieved?   Yes   No

   If there were any revisions please describe them.

   _____

   _____

5. Were the revised goals achieved?   Yes   No

   Please explain.

   _____

   _____

6. Please rate how your partnership developed over time.

   Not Working   Okay   Good   Great

Additional comments:

_____

_____

Closure Meeting
Final Overall Evaluation

Thank you for participating in your organization's Mentoring Partnership Program. In order for us to provide the best experience, we are committed to continuous improvement and this can only be accomplished with your feedback. Please complete the following brief survey.

Please rate the following responses from 1 (not at all effective), 2 (somewhat effective), 3 (neutral), 4 (effective), to 5 (very effective); include brief explanation.

1. Overall, how effective was the mentoring partnership matching process?_____

_____

2. Overall, how effective was the Mentoring Partnership Agreement? _____

_____

3. Overall, how effective was your relationship with your mentoring partner? _____

_____

4. Overall, how effective was the mentoring partnership process in helping you accomplish your learning goals?_____

_____

5. How effective was the overall mentoring partnership experience?_____

_____

Please rate the importance of the following statement: 1 (not at all important), 2 (somewhat important), 3 (neutral), 4 (important), 5 (very important); include brief explanation.

1. Overall, how would you rate the value of the closing celebration? _____

_____

Please briefly answer the following questions.

1. What went well?

_____

_____

_____

2. How can it be improved?

_____

_____

_____

3. Would you recommend the Mentoring Partnership Program to a colleague? Please explain.

Yes   Maybe   No   Don't know

_____

_____

_____

Additional comments:

_____

_____

_____

Chapter 16

The Next Steps: Planning for the Future

This part of the journey may have accomplished your original goals but it is only the beginning. We hope that the process of identifying and building mentoring partnerships either on your own or through an organized program such as the one you are completing has made an impact on your future. This process is a tool that you can use to continue growing and developing personally and professionally.

After completing the six-month rotation, you may be asked to share your experiences and information with other members of your organization or association (to serve as a program ambassador) and to promote the Mentoring Partnership Program. No one can explain the value and benefits as well as someone who has actually participated in the program and can base their presentation on firsthand knowledge.

Long-Term Perspective

In addition to completing an evaluation at the end of your rotation, you may be contacted by the coordinator to participate in a post-program review (it would be around three months after the celebration and closing meeting). The coordinator could use a variety of tools to implement the post-program review, including an electronic feedback form, interviews with a selected group of participants, or a scheduled follow-up discussion session. The purpose of these reviews and assessments is to determine the program's benefits to the participating individuals, the organizations and its ROI.

The Future of Mentoring Partnerships

The authors of this publication plan to continue improving and expanding the Mentoring Partnership Model, as well as updating its resources and tools. To meet our audience's needs and interests and provide quality service, we invite your comments, input, and suggestions. Providing feedback about your experience with the Mentoring Partnership Program will help us learn more about its strengths and discover any shortcomings. You can contact us at mentoringstrategies@gmail.com.

References and Recommended Reading

Alred, G., B. Garvey, and R. Smith. (2008). *Mentoring Pocketbook*. Alresford, Hampshire, UK: Laurel House.

Barnes, A.K. (2011). Breaking Through Generational Stereotypes. *T+D* (June): 30-33.

Benatti, S., and A. Reitman (2012). An Intergenerational Approach to Strengthening Organizational Talent. *T+D* (November): 76-77.

Black, A. (2010). Gen Y: Who They Are and How They Learn. *Educational Horizons* 88(2): 92-101, http://eric.ed.gov/?id=EJ872487.

Carlson, C., and Deloitte & Touche Study. (n.d.) Traditionalists, Baby Boomers, Generation X, Generation Y (and Generation Z) "Working Together": What Matters and How They Learn? How Different are They? Fact and Fiction. United Nations Joint Staff Pension Fund, www.un.org/staffdevelopment/pdf/Designing%20Recruitment,%20Selection%20&%20Talent%20Management%20Model%20tailored%20to%20meet%20UNJSPF's%20Business%20Development%20Needs.pdf.

Cambiano, R.L., J.B. De Vore, and R.L. Harvey. (2001). Learning Style Preferences of the Cohorts: Generation X, Baby Boomers, and the Silent Generation. *PAACE Journal of Lifelong Learning* 10, http://plus50.aacc.nche.edu/Documents/Cambiano2001.pdf.

Casserly, M. (2012). Millennials and Baby Boomers: At Odds or Peas in a Pod? Forbes.com, www.forbes.com/sites/meghancasserly/2012/01/19/millennial-and-baby-boomers-at-odds-or-peas-in-a-pod/.

Emelo, R. (2011a). Who's Sharing Knowledge in Your Organization? *Talent Management* 2013, 20-23. <Query: Was this from 2013 or 2011?>

———. (2011b). Creating a Mindset: Guidelines for Mentorship in Today's Workplace. *T+D* (January): 44-49.

Ensher, E., and S. Murphy. (2005). *Powering mentoring: How successful mentors and protégés get the most out of their relationships.* San Francisco: Jossey-Bass.

Fleming, N., and D. Baume. (2006). Learning Styles Again: Varking Up the Right Tree. Educational Developments, SEDA, 7.4: 4-7, www.vark-learn.com/documents/educational%20developments.pdf.

Forsberg, C. (2010). The Baby Boomer, Gen Y Communications Gap and Social Media…the Solution or the Problem? www.clayforsberg.net/2010/08/28/the-baby-boomer-gen-y-communications-gap-and-social-media-the-solution-or-the-problem/.

Goudreau, J. (2013). How to Communicate in the New Multigenerational Office. Forbes.com, www.forbes.com/sites/jennagoudreau/2013/02/14/how-to-communicate-in-the-new-multigenerational-office/.

Insala. (2012). 7 Things I Wish I knew Before Starting a Mentoring Program. http://insala.com/Articles/Mentoring/7-things-I-wish-I-knew-before-starting-a-mentoring-program.asp.

Johnson, W.B., and C.R. Ridley. (2008). *The Elements of Mentoring.* New York: Palgrave Macmillan.

Kersten, D. (2002). Today's Generations Face New Communication Gaps. USA Today, www.usatoday.com/money/jobcenter/workplace/communication/2002-11-15-communication-gap_x.htm.

Knowles, M.S., and E.F. Holton III. (2005). *The Adult Learner: The Definitive Classic in Adult Education and Human Resource Development.* 6th ed. Burlington, MA: Elsevier.

Kolb, A.Y., and D.A. Kolb. (2011). *Kolb Learning Style Inventory 4.0.* Boston: Hay Group Publishers.

Lawson, K. (2007). *Successful Coaching & Mentoring.* Happauge, NY: Barron's.

Long, M. (2010). Communicating with Baby Boomers, Gen X and Gen Y. *NFP Analysts*, www.nfp.net.au/communicating-with-baby-boomers-gen-x-and-gen-y.html.

Milkint, M.R. (2011). Intergenerational Communications: Baby Boomers, Generation X and Generation Y. *Association Insurance Compliance Professionals (AICP) 2011 Annual Conference.* www.jacobsononline.com/uploadFiles/presentation81.pdf.

Oblinger, D. (2003). Boomers and Gen-Xers and Millenials Understanding the New Students. *Educause.edu*, Retrieved from http://net.educause.edu/ir/library/pdf/erm0342.pdf

Rothewell, W.J. (2008). *Adult Learning Basics.* Alexandria, VA: ASTD Press.

Sandberg, S. (2013). *Lean In: Women, Work, and the Will to Lead.* New York: Alfred A. Knopf.

Theielfoldt, D., and D. Scheef. (2005). Generation X and the Millennials: What You Need to Know About Mentoring the New Generations. *Law Practice Today* (November), http://apps.americanbar.org/lpm/lpt/articles/mgt08044.html.

Ware, J., R. Craft, and S. Kerschenbaum, (n.d.). Training Tomorrow's Workforce. Kreative Learning Solutions, www.kreativelearningsolutions.com/pdfs/VLLeadership/Generational%20Dynamics/Training%20Tomorrow's%20Workforce_ASTD%20Pub.pdf

Way, C., and B. Kaye. (2011). Tools for Effective Mentoring Programs. *Infoline.* Alexandria, VA: ASTD Press.

Zachary, L.J., and L.A. Fischler. (2013). Facilitating Mentee-Driven Goal Setting. *T+D*, April 2013, pp. 76-77

———. (2012a). *Strategies for Mentees. Pocket Toolkit #3*. San Francisco: John Wiley & Sons.

———. (2012b). *Accountability Strategies and Checklists. Pocket Toolkit #4*. San Francisco: John Wiley & Sons.

———. (2012c). *Mentoring Across Generations. Pocket Toolkit #5*. San Francisco: John Wiley & Sons.

———. (2011). Begin with the End in Mind: The Goal-Driven Mentoring Relationship. *T+D* January: 50-53.

Zust, C.W. (n.d.). Baby Boomer Leaders Face Challenges Communicating Across the Generations. Emerging Leaders.com, www.emergingleader.com/article16.shtml.

About the Authors

Annabelle Reitman has over 40 years of experience in career coaching and counseling, specializing in résumé development that targets clients' individualized professional stories as well as short-term coaching for people in work transitions enabling them to successfully continue their career journey. Her tagline, "possibilities without assumptions," summarizes her philosophy and approach to working with people. Reitman is an established writer and author in the career and talent management arenas. Her latest publication (co-authored) is *Career Moves*, 3rd edition, (ASTD Press, 2013). She is a past president and co-president of the ASTD Metro DC Chapter and past president of the Association of Career Professionals International (ACPI) DC Chapter.

Sylvia Ramirez Benatti brings more than 20 years' experience in the nonprofit sector as a trainer, consultant, and university professor in nonprofit management. She has produced and hosted the *Nonprofit Edge*, a weekly interview show on the university's cable station. She co-developed and successfully delivered the Mentoring Partnership Model as a program for the ASTD Metro DC Chapter. Benatti is certified as a Standards of Excellence Consultant and in Quality Matters

Online Teaching. As the director of training for the Support Center of Washington, D.C., she planned, scheduled, published, and managed a full time public training program with an average of 60 workshops per quarter. She holds a doctorate degree in Organizational Leadership in Nonprofits from Nova Southeastern University, and a master's degree in Training & Professional Development from Mount Vernon College, an affiliate school of the George Washington University.